Rachel, a Chilean by birth, a daughter of holocaust survivors, a widow of a physician who committed suicide, a mother of three grown sons, meets a handsome, wealthy American bachelor on a cruise to the Greek Isles. She falls madly in love with the man - her burning bush - and leaves her job, her sons in Spain, her friends, her Spanish culture to follow her gringo to the United States. They embark on a magnificent four-month honeymoon in which they visit Mexico, Venezuela, Brazil, Argentina, Chile, Ecuador, the Amazon, and the Galapagos Islands.

Rachel returns to Spain to visit with her sons while her lover remains in the United States. She abruptly ends the relationship and disappears.

The man is heartbroken. Using his background as a psychologist and industrial spy, he initiates an investigation to locate Rachel and solve the mystery of her behavior. What he discovers is the raison d'être for writing the book.

This book is based on a true story.

RACHEL'S BURNING BUSH

RACHEL'S BURNING BUSH

Heaven has no rage like love turned to hatred.

The story of a man's painful relationship with a "borderline personality"

Lucho ben Alexander

LUVO Publishing

Library of Congress Cataloging-In Publication Information

Alexander, Lucho ben

Rachel's Burning Bush: The story of a man's painful relationship with a "borderline personality" / Lucho ben Alexander

   p. cm.

   Includes bibliographical references.

   ISBN 0-9643782-0-5

   1. Borderline personality disorder. 2. Mentally ill--Biography. 3. Women--Mental health. I. Title

RC569.5.B67B45 1995   616.89'0092   B--dc20   94-96520
   CIP

Rachel's Burning Bush
Copyright 1996 © Lucho ben Alexander

Published by Luvo Publishing	Phone: 617-894-7977
22 Middlesex Circle	Fax: 617-566-9350
Waltham, MA 02154 U.S.A	

All rights reserved. No part of this book may be reproduced or transmitted in any form or by any means, electronic or mechanical.

Disclaimer: While this book is based on a true story, all individual names, company names, and geographical references have been changed to protect the rights of privacy of the people involved. The conclusion offered at the end of the book is stated as an opinion of the author only and not as a fact or definitive diagnosis.

Manufactured in the United States of America.

PREFACE
THE TITLE

In this story the expression "burning bush" is a biblical reference from Exodus in the Old Testament.

Exodus - 3: "And the angel of the Lord appeared to Moses in a flame of fire out of the midst of a bush; and he looked, and lo, the bush was burning, yet it was not consumed. And Moses said, 'I will turn aside and see this great sight, why the bush is not burnt.' When the lord saw that he turned aside to see, God called to him out of the bush, 'Moses, Moses!' And he said, 'Here am I.' Then he said, 'I am the God of your father, the God of Abraham, the God of Isaac, and the God of Jacob.' And Moses hid his face, for he was afraid to look at God."

The burning bush in the title "Rachel's Burning Bush" refers to God.

This is a true story about a relationship I had with a woman called Rachel. I was Rachel's "Burning Bush."

The name Rachel also has some biblical significance. In the bible Jacob worked fourteen years in order to marry Rachel. Like Jacob, I loved Rachel very deeply. This is a story of mutual love.

The title, "Rachel's Burning Bush," with its varied interpretations and meanings, was chosen to set the tone of the story itself. The story, like the title, has a talmudic dimension to it. There is not only an elusive dialectic which exists within the story, but also a subtle nexus which ambulates between some of the discordant parts.

TABLE OF CONTENTS

Preface	The Title	i

Maps:
- Mexico 52
- South America 59

Introduction: Background to The Story 1
Organization of Book 4

Chapter 1: My Background 6
- Overview 6
- Early Life 6
- Retirement 26
- 1990 27
- Florida, January - March 1991 28
- Europe, Fall 1991 28

Chapter 2: Rachel 30
- Meeting Rachel 30
- Rachel's History 33

Chapter 3: Relationship With Rachel 38
- On Board the Omega 38
- Spain, November 1991 40
- Boston, December 1991 43
- My Brother's Death 47
- Florida, January 1992 49
- Mexico 51
- Venezuela 58
- Brazil 61

Table of contents continued

- Iguacu Falls 62
- Argentina 62
- Chile 67
- Ecuador 78
- Amazon 80
- Galapagos Islands 81
- Quito 86
- Florida, March 1992 87
- Virginia 93

Chapter 4: Ending of Relationship 96
- Spain, April 1992 96
- My Emotional Reaction to Rachel's Decision 101
- Letter to Rachel 102
- Reaction of My Brother and Friends To My Letter 112
- Rachel's Reply 114
- Reaction of Friends and Family To Rachel's Letter 115

Chapter 5: Investigation of Rachel 117
- Summer and Fall 1992 117
- Spain, November 1992 119
- Return to Boston, December 1992   127
- Return to Florida, December 1992 . 132
- Letter to Olympus Cruise Line 142
- Letter to Rachel and Her Family .. 143
- Trip to Galveston 144
- Galveston, Texas, March 1993 145

Table of contents continued

- Letter to Captain Washington 153
- Letter to Richard Ward 154
- District Attorney of Galveston 156
- Boston, Spring 1993 157
- Psychotherapy 163
- Sudden Endings - Other Men 165
- Psychologist and Psychiatrists 170
- Private Detectives 176
- Hypnotherapist 180
- Children of Holocaust Survivor 182

Chapter 6:   Conclusion 183

Appendix 187
- Author's Name 188
- Title 189
- Analysis 191

Bibliography 211

INTRODUCTION:

BACKGROUND TO THE STORY

In the winter of my life, I met a woman aboard a Greek cruise ship who brought sunshine into my life. She left her job, her country, her family, and her culture to come with me to the United States. She asked nothing of me. She only wanted to be with me. Her love for me was total and unconditional. Whatever I wanted, wherever I wanted to go, suited her as long as we were together. While we were not legally married, (she never pressed the issue of marriage), she considered herself to be my wife. She manifested obsessional love toward me. She called me her "burning bush." She stated she wanted to spend not only this life with me but all eternity and be buried with me. She quoted from the book of Ruth in the Bible (Ruth 1:16): "Your God shall be my God; your people shall be my people; where you go, I will go; where you lodge, so shall I; where you die, I will die, and there will I be buried."

We spent from mid November 1991 to mid April 1992 together.

During this period I developed a sense of oneness with her and complete trust. I experienced inner harmony. Feeling totally secure in the relationship, I opened my heart to this woman as I had done to no other. I loved and gave love openly and without reservation.

I thought of Proverbs 31: "A good wife who can

find? She is far more precious than jewels. The heart of her husband trusts in her, and he will have no lack of gain. She does him good, and not harm, all the days of her life."

In the winter of my life I had found peace and love. A sense of well being filled me.

Rachel was her name. In mid April of 1992 she returned to her home in Spain to be with her family. She had a round-trip ticket to return in a month. I remained in the United States for medical tests.

Within two weeks of returning to Spain, she told me she intended to remain in Spain and end our relationship. I no longer existed for her. It was like I was a stranger. I was bewildered. I couldn't understand what had happened. How was it possible for a woman to switch from a state of obsessional love to never wanting to see her love object again without any intervening event? It didn't make any sense. I was confused, angry and hurt. I experienced great emotional pain and angst. It was as if someone had ripped apart my insides.

This book represents my attempt to explain or understand Rachel's behavior. It is painful for me to write. I am a private individual and take no delight in telling this story. It reflects poorly on me. I have gone out of my way to focus on my own psychopathology in order to provide insight into the dynamics of the relationship and attempt to present the relationship from Rachel's point of view. Rachel and her family

BACKGROUND TO THE STORY

were given an outline of the story and solicitated to rebut the facts. They chose not to do so.

I am writing for the following heuristic reasons: (1) The subject of male emotional pain needs to be more fully acknowledged and addressed. Much of male behavior germinates from such pain. (2) The fact that men are sometimes victims, not always perpetrators, needs to be recognized. (3) Mental-health professionals need to understand the symptoms and the psychodynamics described in this story in order to help their patients, whether victim or perpetrator. (4) The psychodynamics of male and female development needs to be understood by both sexes.

What prompted me to write the book was that almost every psychiatrist and psychologist who had read a summary of this story was baffled. Each of them recognized psychiatric diagnostic features in Rachel but found there was too much inconsistency to fit any one diagnosis. With the exception of one therapist, not one of the professionals with whom I consulted had ever heard a story quite like this. They had heard parts of the story before, but nothing like the whole story. Of the countless friends and family members to whom I have told the story, none had ever heard a story like it either. Only some of the professional writers of fiction with whom I have spoken have claimed to have heard a similar story and had insight into the character of Rachel.

I do not believe I have had a unique experience.

RACHEL'S BURNING BUSH

I suspect many men have had similar experiences. Masculine pride, reluctance to speak of emotional pain and feelings, bewilderment, sense of powerlessness, embarrassment at being a victim—all may have contributed to male silence. It is time to light a candle!

ORGANIZATION OF THE BOOK

This book is about a relationship. The first part is autobiographical, followed by a background of Rachel, details of our relationship and its ending, my subsequent investigation of Rachel, and finally an analysis and conclusion based on my findings.

The investigation of Rachel took me on a life journey—which constitute a major part of the book—with unexpected twists and turns; plot and subplots; acts, scenes, and characters. At one point I came very close to being thrown in jail. Out of this bedlam, clarity and insight surfaced, which I share with the reader.

The analysis and conclusion are psychologically oriented and based on the facts uncovered, my discussions with professionals in the field, my extensive readings of the literature, and my own personal experience. The conclusion is consistent with current theory in psychology and psychiatry.

The appendix contains a more detailed and polemical analysis and discussion than found in the main body of the book. It is directed to the mental-

BACKGROUND TO THE STORY

health professional.

CHAPTER 1: MY BACKGROUND

OVERVIEW

At the time I met Rachel, I was fifty-seven and Rachel was fifty. I had never been married although I never lacked for female companionship for any length of time. My father had been a dentist, and my mother had been a housewife with a law degree. My parents had three sons. I was the oldest. My middle brother, Julio, was three-years younger and my youngest brother, Esteban, was eight years my junior.

EARLY LIFE

My early life was eventful. On my mother's side, I was the first-born grandson and carry the first name of my maternal grandfather. I was treated like a little God. As was the custom in the depression years, and in first-generation Americans, my family lived in close proximity to other family members. I enjoyed the love and camaraderie of my maternal grandmother, aunts, uncles, and cousins. Though my childhood bridged the years of the Second World War, I remained untouched by the events of those turbulent years. No member of my family died in the war. I experienced the war through news reels on Saturday afternoon at the movies.

My father was a self-made man. My paternal grandfather had died walking with my father on the way to my dad's Bar Mitzvah (age thirteen). My

MY BACKGROUND

paternal grandmother went out and sold flowers on the street to support her family. To help support the family as well as further his education, my dad sold newspapers on the streets of Boston. He obtained a scholarship to Harvard and graduated from their dental school. He worked very hard as a dentist, and the only time I saw him was in the morning before school and on Sunday. He was a kind, happy, calm, strong, confident, secure gentleman with eclectic knowledge. He liked to tease—especially his nieces. He did well financially as a dentist, and many of the Boston elite were among his patients. Also among his patients were those who could not afford to pay anything. I was sorry that he had to work so hard and rarely enjoyed playing with his children. He was my idol.

My mother was a beautiful woman, with blond hair, and a slim figure. She had the capacity to evoke a sense of awe in men. In contrast to my dad, my mother led a pampered existence as the youngest daughter of a wealthy businessman. She was driven around by the family chauffeur. When she graduated from law school at the age of twenty, she was too young to sit for the bar exam. She never practiced law. After she married my father, she became a housewife. That is the way family life was in the nineteen thirties. My mother was on the shy side and did not flaunt her beauty. I think she recognized it as an asset, and she was very good at manipulating men to realize her goals. From my mother I learned neatness, civility and proper manners, responsibility, the importance of hard work, to fight for my rights, to strive to be the best, and respect for women and my elders. My mother took her job of wife and mother very seriously. Her family was her life. She was the rock in my life—someone on whom I could always count.

The third important person in my life was my maternal grandmother—whom I called Bubbie (yiddish for grandmother). She was born in Russia and lived her life as an orthodox Jew. She was a woman of grace and piety. God and family were her life. Love for her children and grandchildren filled her heart. I remember her as a woman of pure goodness. I loved her very much.

She was the most noble and unselfish person I ever knew. I consider her to be in a class by herself. (Rachel and my bubbie appeared to share many common traits. That's the level of trust and high opinion I had in Rachel.)

When I was about two years old, my parents separated for a short time. We were living with my bubbie in her house. My father wanted to establish his own home, but my mother and her brothers felt it was my mother's responsibility—as the youngest daughter—to stay with her mother. A rift developed between my dad and my mom's brothers over this issue. Words were exchanged and enmity developed. My dad finally

MY BACKGROUND

left and went to Florida on vacation. While he was there, I became seriously ill with rheumatic fever. This prompted my dad to return. After I recovered, my bubbie told my mother that her place was with her husband, and we moved out within a year.

My boyhood was happy and carefree. I was all boy. Sports rather than school or reading were my main interests. I loved to play tackle football where I could smash into people or tackle them. I was wild, full of energy, joyful, aggressive, fearless and fearsome. I drove my mother crazy. She couldn't control me. Her solution was to put me to bed for the night by late afternoon so she could enjoy some peace.

Beginning probably around the age of six, I expressed an interest in the "facts of life." I would ask my mother who would tell me to see my father. My father would tell me to wait until I had my Bar Mitzvah. This interest continued unabated until the age of ten when I was enlightened by the boys in the street. I attribute my adult insatiable curiosity about life and the need to know as stemming from this early sexual curiosity which was frustrated.

For the most part I lived the care-free existence of the first-born son of an upper-middle-class dentist in an affluent suburb of Boston. Even during the war years we had butter and steak on our table. My dad's "B" gas sticker allowed us some freedom to travel. My mother took me clothes' shopping at the exclusive stores for the wealthy.

RACHEL'S BURNING BUSH

In 1943 my father had a heart attack. In January 1945, when I was ten years old, my father died from a second heart attack. He was forty-one. One month later in February, his mother (my grandmother) was shot to death in a holdup in a pawn shop she owned. In April FDR died. In May Germany surrendered, and the full extent of the Holocaust became known. In August the atomic bombs were dropped on Japan. On Thanksgiving Day my maternal grandmother died from pancreatic cancer.

I remember the year 1945 as the year of death.

Two of the most important people in my life died: My father was a source of strength, and my maternal grandmother was a source of unconditional love. As I entered puberty, these two support systems were no longer available.

In that one year I went from boyhood, through puberty and adolescence, into adulthood— philosophically at least. While my classmates played sports, I pondered existential matters. I delved into religion, psychology, and philosophy. The carefree days of boyhood were over. The weight of the world was on my shoulders. It was made clear to me that I was alone; I had no father; and if I was to make it in this world, I would have to do it on my own. I developed a focused discipline which has never left me.

I remember not being allowed to visit my father in the hospital. Children were not allowed. I remember not being allowed to go to my father's

MY BACKGROUND

funeral or to the cemetery—I was considered too young. Again the adult world frustrated my need to know and come to closure. But paradoxically I assumed the adult responsibility of saying the mourner's kaddish for my father (the prayer for the dead in the Jewish religion—actually a reaffirmation of your belief in God despite your grief.)

The above events had an impact on my developing personality. The decision by well-meaning but misguided adults to keep me from visiting my father in the hospital or attending his funeral has fueled potentially explosive anger later in life toward authority figures who enforce the law, or rules and regulations, without understanding or reasonableness. These actions by adults kept me in a benighted state vis-à-vis my father and together with earlier unanswered sexual questions served to drive my insatiable intellectual appetite.

After my father died, my maternal grandmother came to live with us. Within a few months, she became ill and spoke with her three sons. She was concerned about Gerty (my mother's name was Gertrude) and the three young boys (myself and my two younger brothers). She asked her two oldest sons to provide financial assistance to Gerty and her boys. (My father's brothers had predeceased him.) She asked her youngest son, who was a bachelor, to stay with us and make sure Gerty was not alone. The love my uncles had for their mother was absolute. Her request was implemented without question. Within a few years, my bachelor uncle married. Mindful of the request of his mother, the oldest son enjoined his teenage daughter to live with us. She did so until she graduated from high school. The close-knit-extended-family was something I accepted as natural. I internalized this and assumed a protective and responsible attitude to my mother and younger brothers. Later in life, my brothers would occasionally object to my big brother attitude. They were too young when my father died to understand the forces that shaped my personality.

My uncles' financial assistance created a dilemma for me. I had been unaware of the schism between my father and my uncles. A few months after my father's death, an older female cousin informed me about the hard feelings that existed between my dad and my mother's brothers. I did not know at the time that my cousin's comments were generated by the ill-will that existed between her father and my mother's brothers arising out of a business venture. It was a cruel and thoughtless act my cousin did and caused irreparable harm to me. I loved my father. My pain from his death was very deep. His friends were my friends; his enemies were my enemies. And now I was forced to accept financial assistance from his enemies. My uncles tried, especially my middle uncle who had a son my age, to be nice to me. This uncle in many ways treated me like a son. When it came time for my

MY BACKGROUND

Bar Mitzvah, he arranged for me to have a double Bar Mitzvah with his son; and the magnificent party later was a joint affair. Out of allegiance to my father, I remained respectful but cool and distant to my uncles. A boy needs older males to identify with, to talk with, to seek counsel from, to learn about women, to learn about the world of men. As I went from puberty to adolescence, this lack of an adult male role model made the transitional years all the more difficult. My mother continued to be a strong influence on my life and her Weltanschauung became mine. But her outlook was that of a woman, and a man must walk a different road. This caused an internal struggle within me which has abated over the years but still exists. I compete with and discuss facts with men, but I talk and share feelings with women. The result is a man with a mind and body, restless intellect and competitive spirit, physical drives and psychological desires of a man; but the gentle and compassionate soul of a woman.

For almost six years, until I was able to drive, I lived in a sort of dream world, not being sure about my father's death. Only when I was able to drive and visit the cemetery did I accept my father's death. Only then did the psychological pain begin to lift.

My world changed abruptly after my father died. My father had been the strength and unifying force in the family. We went from a spendthrift to a penurious life style. Hamburgers and spaghetti became the mainstay of our nightly dinners. Clothes' shopping at discount and basement stores became the rule. The family unit became both close and filled with tension. Trauma or major stress tends to do that. My mother and I fought a lot, although we remained very close.

My mother and I were both in great pain from my father's death. I "acted out" and became a difficult child. My mother in turn took out her frustrations on me. She made it clear to me that I was a bad son, a bad boy, and no one really liked me. "How could anyone like someone who is bad to his mother," she would say. When boys would come over to the house to ask me to play football, she would tell me: "They are not interested in you, but your football." One of her expressions I remember clearly: "Life will not be good for you until you are good to your mother." It was because of my mother's attitude toward me that I became very sensitive to rejection and suspicious of the motives of others toward me.

My mother was high strung and kept a spotless house. Cleanliness, orderliness, and doing everything on time were her fetish. After my father's death, my mother's personality ruled our house. It was a rough assignment to be widowed at thirty-five and left with three boys—ages ten, six and one. To my mother's credit, she devoted her life to raising her boys and did without personal pleasures. There was very little insurance money—I believe a monthly check from Prudential for seventy-two dollars (later raised to

MY BACKGROUND

seventy-eight dollars) plus some assistance from her brothers for about five years. Thank goodness the house was paid for. I do not know how my mother did it, but we survived. Her frugality and smart shopping pulled us through. Only when her three sons were educated and her youngest son was in college did my mother go to work. She was fifty-five years old when she re-entered the workforce. She worked for ten years in a clerical/statistical capacity and retired on full social security benefits. When she died in 1990, she left an estate valued at almost six hundred thousand dollars. She had accomplished this on her own by saving and wise investments while at the same time seeing to it that her children were educated. I became an entrepreneur, my middle brother an electrical engineer, and my youngest brother an attorney. The three of us owe much to her.

My father's death produced lasting long-term changes in my personality. On the one hand I developed a strong, autonomous, disciplined, competitive, high-need-to-achieve personality. I refer to this as my male self. On the other hand the emotional pain I experienced produced what I call a female self. I have a soft, sensitive, gentle, tender, caring, empathetic personality. The two personalities are well-integrated. I stand erect and my body language is one of confidence and comfort. I am relaxed and calm and have a soft gentle voice. When I speak with someone, I maintain eye contact. I am happy and upbeat when I am with people and am also happy and content when being alone. I project the qualities of a gentleman of high integrity and honesty. My integrated personality can fragment however and depending on the circumstances either the male or female self can surface. If I feel threatened or attacked, my male persona is energized. On the other hand I am particularly sensitive to another person's pain and in such a case my female persona surfaces. It was my female side which was touched by Rachel's poignant life history. She did not stimulate my male sexual drive, but rather she evoked the emotion of compassion from within my female personality. Later you will see it was my female persona coupled with my gentlemanly qualities which Rachel found irresistible. The male personality which surfaced later was her bête noire.

  The pain from all these losses in 1945 had an immediate and lasting impact on my personality. I became withdrawn and introspective, very careful about money, and concerned what would happen to me and my brothers if something happened to my mother. As the eldest male in the house, I developed a sense of being responsible for my mother and brothers. While I was only ten, in some respects I became like a man of forty. The fun of childhood disappeared, and the responsibilities for manhood were thrust on my shoulders—at least psychologically. One of the decisions I made was never to become too close

MY BACKGROUND

to anyone, and thereby I would avoid pain from someone dying and leaving me. The is one of the reasons I never married.

There are probably other reasons as well. For some reason I equated marriage with death and loss of freedom (rather than a rebirth), of being closed in without escape, a trap. I saw children as a burden and responsibility (rather than a joy and opportunity). I saw women entering marriage never for just love but to have a Mrs. in front of their name, to have someone take care of them financially, to have children, and to use a man's strength as a crutch to compensate for their weakness and low self-esteem. I have often noticed the reluctance of women to remarry once they have financial independence and have had children. I have always walked away when a woman pressed for marriage, since I felt they were less interested in me and building a life together than they were in marriage. (Rachel was the only woman who penetrated my Maginot Line. She asked nothing of me.)

During my adolescent years, my mother told a story about a Jewish-mother's love. She related how a son met the devil in the center of town. The devil told the son if he would bring his mother's heart to him, the son would have whatever he desired in life. The world would be his. The son went home, cut out his mother's heart, placed it in a shoe box, and ran down the front steps. In his haste to get to the devil, the son fell and the box and heart slipped from his hands. The mother's heart, having fallen onto the pavement, said: "Did you hurt yourself son?" My mother ended the story by saying that is what a Jewish mother is, and there is no love like a mother's love.

My mother saw herself in this way. Her love and devotion were actually a double-edged sword. She couldn't let go of her sons and made it difficult for her sons to let go of her. Any woman would have a tough time competing with this. My mother had set some difficult standards for a woman to meet. Any woman I met was unconsciously compared to the mother in this story. (Only Rachel had met these impossible standards.)

Sometime in my adolescent years I began to develop a slight tremor in my hands. This tremor became noticeable whenever I had to read something before a group of people, drink anything from a glass, or extend my arm to light a girl's cigarette. While most prominent in my right hand, the tremor was bilateral. The hand tremor was accompanied by a slight voice tremor. It became socially embarrassing and fed on itself: the psychological discomfort of people looking at me and thinking I was nervous only made me more nervous and the tremor increased.

My first year in college was a disappointment.

At the end of my first semester, I received a failing grade in French. I was devastated. I had never failed a course in my life. The Ivy League University I attended required that each student demonstrate

MY BACKGROUND

proficiency in a foreign language. The professor in the course indicated that if I repeated the course, I would fail it again. When that happened, I would be prohibited from taking any foreign languages at the university.

I contacted members of the administration to obtain a variance from the language requirement. I was told that if I didn't like the system, I was free to leave.

Finally, one day I spoke to the Assistant Dean. He agreed with me that the requirement was antediluvian. In light of what my professor had indicated about my chance of passing the course, the regulation seemed inane. He told me that I didn't have to take the course the next semester, and he would write this in my record. I didn't have to take it the following year either. He couldn't do anything about the requirement however. Unless the faculty voted to rescind the rule, I would have to, at some point, fulfill the requirement. He left it up to me. It was my decision. He would support me whatever I did. He suggested that I consider taking the course the next semester, putting it behind me, and enjoying the rest of my college years. If I postponed taking the course, I would have it hanging over me. He suggested that I think about it and do whatever I felt was in my best interest.

I took the course the next semester, failed it, and went on to enjoy the rest of my college years.

RACHEL'S BURNING BUSH

The Assistant Dean went on to become the Dean of the University and finally accepted a position as president of another university.

This was one of the most enduring educational experiences I had at college. It taught me the importance of listening to another person, validating another person's position and feelings, putting yourself into another person's shoes, and reaching an agreement which is in the best interest of the other party. A person wins only in a win-win scenario. Any other scenario is a loss for both parties. If you win and the other party loses, then you both lose in the long run. A person does not win by promoting his ideas and demeaning the ideas of others. You control others by allowing a person to believe he is in control. Only then can you move a person to your position. The Dean was a man of rare wisdom.

I went on to receive my A.B. and M.A. in psychology and then entered an M.B.A. program—all at Ivy-League Schools. I have published a number of research articles in journals of both clinical and physiological psychology.

When I was in my early twenties, I consulted a neurologist about my tremor. He advised me that the tremor was psychological since it was bilateral. He told me that a neurological tremor would generally be on one side only.

Since the tremor seemed to be people related, I went to a psychiatrist who specialized in group

MY BACKGROUND

therapy. He in turn sent me to a psychologist who specialized in projective tests. I found the psychologist's written report to the psychiatrist interesting. She wrote that when she began to evaluate my responses, her initial thoughts were that I was psychotic. The quantity and variety of responses, especially to the color segments, were more than she had ever seen. A large number of responses above the average was generally associated with psychosis. On more careful evaluation however, she realized that my responses reflected a man of high intelligence who had eclectic interests. I was very logical and reality based. The sensitivity to color was a manifestation of my feeling nature. I was essentially a passive man, but I could be very dangerous if I felt threatened. There was a possibility of physical violence under these circumstances. I thought her analysis was on the mark. I spent close to two years in group and individual psychotherapy to overcome this social tremor. The tremor did not abate.

My first job after business school was as a commercial spy. I was euphemistically called a market research analyst and the department I worked in was referred to as the commercial intelligence department. I was involved in product and market planning for the company and to this end used overt and covert investigatory procedures. Later on, when I investigated Rachel, I utilized some of the techniques learned during my days of spying.

RACHEL'S BURNING BUSH

Most of my career was spent as an entrepreneur in the electronics' field. I was granted a patent in electro-optics. I worked sixteen hours a day, seven days a week. My workaholic schedule was not a labor of love. Operating my company was a struggle and full of frustration. My business drive was predicated on not being a loser rather than building an empire. Losing was an anathema to me! It took me almost seven years before the corporation generated a positive cash flow. For a few years after that, the business was a cash cow. I consider myself a failure as a businessman. Most of my money was made from investing in stocks—chiefly utility stocks. My major investment appreciated over six-fold in less than ten years. It was this investment which provided me with my financial independence.

When I was in my mid-thirties, I developed back problems and was sent to a neurosurgeon for evaluation of a slipped disc. He recommended against surgery. He told me, however, that my tremor was called essential or familial tremor and was a neurological problem. In addition to my hand and voice tremor, there was a slight tremor in my face and diaphragm. This particular tremor would be exacerbated by psychological or physical stress and reduced by drinking alcohol. There was no known medical treatment for it. (This was 1974.) All those years I had thought this tremor was a symptom of deep psychological problems!

MY BACKGROUND

In 1981, at the age of forty-seven, I had my first heart attack.

When I was admitted to the hospital, I asked someone to call my office and tell them I would not be in for a few days. Someone in my company called my brother Esteban. Esteban then called the hospital and spoke to the attending cardiologist. He told Esteban that he wasn't sure of the diagnosis and told Esteban to call back in a few hours. Esteban left his office—telling his staff that his brother was in the hospital—and drove over to my mother's apartment.

When Esteban arrived at my mother's apartment, he explained what he knew and suggested they wait and call the physician in a few hours. My mother looked at him as if he was crazy. "Lucho is in the hospital and you expect me to wait here," she said. "I don't even know how to get to the suburb he lives in, let alone the hospital. But I am not staying here. If Lucho is in the hospital, that is where I am going." Esteban took my mother to the hospital. (Those of you who are parents can, I am sure, identify with my mother's emotions.)

I alerted the cardiologist to the fact that my mother was a widow. My father had died from a heart attack, and there was a cardiovascular disease on his side of the family. My mother had devoted her life to raising her three sons. She would be in a state of high anxiety. I asked him to be extra sensitive to her needs and concerns.

RACHEL'S BURNING BUSH

When I saw my mother approaching my room, I purposely raised my arm and waved to her— indicating I was okay. I wanted to allay her fears. She and Esteban both entered my room. The nurses and cardiologists were in and out of my room every few minutes and my mother and Esteban were finally asked to leave and allow me to rest.

I remember the first night clearly. I was frightened but still feisty. They tried to sedate me so that I would sleep, but I was too hyped up. If I was going to die, I wanted to die with my eyes open and still fighting. I didn't want to die in my sleep without a final fight. I allowed myself to go to sleep only when the first rays of sunlight became visible. I had made it through eighteen hours and felt the greatest danger was over.

When I awoke in the early afternoon, my family was at my bedside. I told them I was very angry at my heart. It had let me down. I had been on a low-fat diet and exercised regularly. I had pampered my heart. Now it was going to pay for what it did to me. I would punish it. I would lead an ascetic existence and follow a stringent diet and exercise regimen. I wanted my heart to suffer.

This is an example of what in Yiddish is called talking like a meshuggener. Meshuggener means crazy. It doesn't mean insane or psychotic but "crazy-like," "off the wall," illogical, or aberrant. It is a condition of short duration exhibited by otherwise

MY BACKGROUND

normal functioning people. The term can be used with affection or can be used to demean. The English equivalent might be "nutty like a fruit cake."

People respond differently to having a heart attack. There is a group of men, small in number, who take control of their lives. They listen to their cardiologist; they read extensively about heart disease. They view their physicians as medical consultants rather than icons. They chart their own path to recovery. Such patients often outlive their predictable survival rate. Paradoxically, their type "A" personalities, which contributed to their heart disease to begin with, now becomes the key to their survival.

I fell into this group. I was obsessed with regaining my health. Nothing or no one could stop me from realizing my goal. It wasn't that I wanted to win, but I just didn't want to lose. I felt if I could "make it" for six months, the ball would be in my court. The trauma to my heart and body would have reached a homeostatic level; the advantage would be mine and I would never yield it.

This obsessive drive, this undaunted tenacity, characterized by a friend as acting like a general without an army, would resurface later as I pursued my investigation of Rachel.

I had enough money to retire after my first heart attack, but I felt the business had more potential and wanted to see it through to the next level. The heart attack really had weakened me. It took me five months before I could return to work on a part-time basis and almost two years to regain my strength.

Five years later, in 1986, I had a second heart attack. The second heart attack prompted me to sell my business and retire. In 1987 I had extensive coronary-bypass surgery.

My mother was the main support system I had during these various medical crises. After both heart attacks and bypass surgery, I convalesced at her apartment. She gave up her bed and slept on the sofa in her living room.

RETIREMENT

The first year of retirement, 1987, was spent recovering from bypass surgery. While some people recover quickly from this surgery, I experienced a great deal of discomfort (the scar is still sore eight years later) and a slow recovery. I spent the years 1988-1989 attending to matters I had always wanted to do. I did a lot of reading for pleasure, bought a condo in Florida, traveled extensively throughout the United States, and restored the cemetery in which my father and bubbie were buried. In 1989 I had some prostate problems. A biopsy was negative but showed a benign hypertrophied prostate—not uncommon in a man my age. In 1989, I began a relationship with a woman which lasted about a year. As the relationship began to unravel, I experienced an existential crisis. Up to

MY BACKGROUND

this time in my life, I had filled my time with school, work, travel, and female companionship. With the disappearance of these activities, I faced a void in my life. Living alone, concerned about the slow deterioration in my heart, without my support systems to challenge me, I turned inward. Depression set in. It fed on itself. At times I would experience a black cloud begin to envelope me. When it came, I fought it. I tightened my fist for combat, thrust my jaw out in preparation to attack, and silently screamed at it to get away from me. The blackness then went away. My depression would lift if I was with people in a friendly social situation or I had some intellectual challenging task. At night, when I was alone, the depression returned. I generally awoke early in the morning—probably around 2:00 A.M.— with a feeling of angst. I coped with the angst by physical activity. I went out for a vigorous walk for a few hours. By mid-morning the depression and angst usually had lifted.

1990

1990 was a terrible year for me. It started with the break up in the relationship I had with the above mentioned woman and ended with my mother's death from pancreatitis (bursting of the pancreas).

RACHEL'S BURNING BUSH

FLORIDA, JANUARY - MARCH 1991

About three weeks after my mother died, I returned to Florida. It was a difficult period for me. I was alone and had no support systems. I developed what I refer to as agitated depression and sought psychiatric help.

EUROPE, FALL 1991

In September and October of 1991 I took a trip to Europe. I traveled alone and was still depressed from my mother's death. I visited England, Holland, France, Italy, and Germany. The end of the trip was a cruise to the Greek Isles and a visit to Turkey.

I was originally scheduled to sail on a ship called the Piraeus owned by Olympus Cruise in Greece. This was their flagship. When I was in Greece, I was advised that the cruise had been changed and offered either my money back or a change to their smaller ship —Omega. If I chose the Omega, I would get a small refund. The original seven-day cruise would be broken up into two cruises: one four day and one three day. I opted for the Omega.

When I boarded the ship, the other passengers were in an angry mood. Like myself, they had been advised of the change at the last moment. In most cases their trip had been planned for many months. Going on a cruise is expensive, and I am sure no one

MY BACKGROUND

would have chosen the option they felt forced to choose. My own attitude was to make the best out of a bad situation. Nothing was to be gained by becoming angry.

CHAPTER 2: RACHEL

MEETING RACHEL

It was on this cruise ship that I met Rachel, who was a social hostess on the ship. Initially, I did not notice her at all, but she noticed me. She was attracted to my gentlemanly carriage and manner as well as my calmness in the midst of the bedlam of irate passengers boarding the ship.

I am tall, a little bit over six feet, stand erect with broad shoulders and full chest, and weigh one hundred eighty-five pounds. The abdominal sinewy of my halcyon youth has been replaced by love handles; the restless stance of earlier days has given way to a middle-aged, deliberate gentlemanly posture, and the hesitant speech of my jeunesse dorée has been supplanted by a rhetoric of quiet confidence. I have brown hair with a speck of gray visible on my sideburns and a bald spot at the crown of my head.

Rachel was intrigued and checked my passport for my name, cabin number, and room arrangement. Satisfied I was traveling alone, she went down to the lower deck where my room was; and as I was coming out of my room she introduced herself. She asked if I was Jewish, indicated she was also, and inquired if I would be interested in seeing a Jewish synagogue when we made our first disembarkment. I said I would and thought nothing more of it. Her job as social hostess was to be nice to passengers.

We spent a lovely time together when we

disembarked. In the synagogue we spoke to a female caretaker who asked if we were married. Making light banter, I put my arm around Rachel and asked the caretaker if she thought Rachel would make a good wife. Rachel, apparently taking this as indicating I was seriously considering marriage, invited me back to her house in Spain. This was the first of many perceptions on her part which later on in our relationship led me to affectionately characterize her as the president of the Vilda Meshuggener Society. (Vilda means wild in Yiddish and just emphasizes the word meshuggener.) During this first encounter she laughed with pleasure, and her eyes frequently filled with tears of happiness. She mentioned it had been a long time since she had laughed.

During the cruise I continued to have a friendly relationship with Rachel. There was no physical contact; in fact she made a point of avoiding physical contact with me. She appeared to be always watching me, especially when I spoke with other women.

Of all the traits which stand out, Rachel's habit of staring at me seemed to be the most unusual. Throughout our relationship, her eyes were always on me. We could be in different parts of a room talking to different people, and Rachel would have her eyes on me. It was as if she was obsessed with me. This behavior was noted by others as well.

Rachel's behavior on board the ship was pleasant; she smiled easily, had a sparkle in her eyes, and was on the shy side. The only makeup she wore was eye makeup. Her hair was arranged in an unflattering manner. (While I was on board, she had her hair styled and cut; and she took on a more attractive appearance.) Her clothes were non-stylish. She had a peculiar walk, much like a peasant woman or a woman accustomed to hard physical work. Her movement or walk was not comfortably integrated as if she felt an awkwardness about her body. She was embarrassed about her English. (I found her English understandable and saw no reason to be embarrassed.) In fact she spoke six languages: English, Spanish, French, Italian, German and Catalan (spoken in Barcelona). She also had a limited knowledge of Greek. This impressed me since foreign languages have been my bête noire.

She worked very hard on the ship and never complained. She was well liked by the passengers. When another staff member would ask her to do something or a passenger would ask her for something, she would run rather than walk to complete the task. She had a servile and insecure manner about her, definitely a follower not a leader—even among the female staff. On the other hand she was no one's fool. If she didn't want to do something, she didn't do it. If a superior spoke to her in anger, and Rachel felt the anger was unjustified, she would not hesitate to show anger back. Because she was such a good worker and pleasant person, this behavior was tolerated.

RACHEL

RACHEL'S HISTORY

Rachel spoke candidly about her past. Her parents were Jewish, came from Austria and Czechoslovakia, fled the Nazis in the late 1930's and came to Chile. The United States immigration policies at that time were not receptive to Jews fleeing the Nazis. Chile, as well as a few other South American countries, accepted the fleeing Jews. Within a short time of her parents' flight to Chile, word was received that the rest of the family had been killed.

Rachel's parents settled in Concepcion which is in the southern part of Chile. A small group of exiled Jews and their children still live in Concepcion. Here, Rachel, and her older sister Leah, were born. Their home was small but comfortable. They lived a middle-class existence. Her father initially owned a bookstore and was modestly successful. He sold the bookstore and with a partner went into farming. This venture failed. Rachel appeared to have a closer relationship with her father than her mother. She reported being beaten by her mother and stubbornly refusing to yield to her mother's demands.

Rachel graduated from high school. Her first husband was a Rabbi. The marriage did not last very long. She claimed her husband had beaten her, locked her in her room and suffered from priapism (prolonged penile erection). This was probably a distortion of reality since priapism is a very painful condition and requires medical treatment within a few hours of onset.

She returned to her parents' home after her first marriage. About five years later, when she was in her mid-twenties, she married again. Her second husband, Georgio, was a physician, of the Catholic faith, and light skinned. Three sons were born from this marriage. Rachel is five feet two inches. Her husband was about five feet five inches. The two oldest boys are about five feet five inches and light-skinned. The youngest boy is at least six feet tall and dark-skinned. He doesn't look at all like his brothers, and temperamentally and intellectually he also differs from them. I wondered about his paternity.

Her husband's family was from Santiago. His parents, brother and sister-in-law, still live there. Rachel reported that she and her husband had a home in Temuco which is in southern Chile. For a number of years early in their marriage they lived on some of the smaller islands off the coast of southern Chile where her husband was the sole physician on the island.

Rachel's husband was a socialist and supported the Allende regime. In September 1973 Allende was overthrown and Pinochet assumed power. The Pinochet regime was anti-communist and trampled on human rights. Rachel's husband was imprisoned for being a socialist and threatened with execution. During the time he was imprisoned, Rachel reported

RACHEL

doing without food for herself in order to bring food to her husband. She was initially prevented by the Pinochet regime from working. They subsequently relented, and she obtained a job (or went into business for herself) delivering ninety-pound gas tanks which she carried on her back. This was quite a task for a woman only five feet two inches tall and maybe one hundred twenty pounds. After a while she hired a young man to help her.

With the help of a lawyer, who took everything they owned, Rachel's husband was able to leave Chile and go to Germany on a medical fellowship. The family left Chile in January 1975. While in Germany Rachel went to school to become a kindergarten teacher.

In 1979, leaving her husband and two oldest children in Germany, Rachel took her youngest son to Spain. She reported she felt uncomfortable as a Jew living in Germany in view of what had happened to the Jews and her family during the Second World War. This was a unilateral decision on the part of Rachel and not a family decision. In 1980 her husband and the two-oldest children joined her in Spain.

The move to Spain was not without its difficulties. Rachel worked only a few months of the year as a tour guide on an ad-libitum basis. Her husband was unable to find work for over a year. The family finances went to almost zero. Finally, in 1981, her husband obtained a low-paying job in medical research (about $27,000 per year). [This decision to move to Spain appears to have been impulsive, narcissistic, and poorly thought through on the part of Rachel. On the other hand, it may have simply reflected underlying problems in the marriage.] In any case it split the family and caused financial hardship.

According to Rachel the marriage was in name only, and she and Georgio slept apart. She claimed her husband was unfaithful. [In retrospect I wonder if this was projection on her part.] In January 1987 her husband committed suicide by hanging. Rachel told me his body or ashes were buried in Santiago, Chile. She also told me that Georgio's suicide was based on his discovering latent-homosexual feelings during the course of psychotherapy. She told someone else the reason had to do with threats from his socialist friends in Chile.

Following her husband's suicide, the family went to Chile for a short while and then visited with Rachel's sister in Virginia before returning to Spain. Rachel reported experiencing depression for three years after her husband's death. During this period she reported consulting a psychologist. She worked "on and off" as a tour guide until the summer of 1991 when she took a job as a telephone operator on the Iliad owned by the Olympus Cruise Company.

She spoke of problems between herself and her sons. Two of the oldest boys had left home because of Rachel's anger and bickering over money. Rachel felt

RACHEL

her sons were spendthrifts and did not realize the dire financial condition of the family. The oldest son, Isaac, subsequently returned home. The middle son, Jacob, struck out on his own and went to France and Syria to study and work. He was financially independent from Rachel.

Rachel reported that her eldest son, when he was younger, commented to her that he didn't ask to be brought into the world, and it was her responsibility to take care of her children.

In 1990 she left her sons at home and, with a group of Jews from Barcelona, went to Israel during the Iraq-mideast war. She had a support rather than a combat position. While in Israel, she met a married American with whom she had an affair. She continued communicating with him until she met me.

CHAPTER 3: RELATIONSHIP WITH RACHEL

ON BOARD THE OMEGA

When I met Rachel in October 1991 on the Omega, she had been promoted to assistant social hostess. Her three sons were eighteen, twenty-two, and twenty-three years old. The youngest was a junior in high school. The other two were juniors in college.

On board the ship my attitude toward the staff was that they all were running away from something. It seemed to me to be on board a ship for five months at a time was an unnatural existence for both male and female staff members. I became aware of sexual liaisons between members of the staff as well as between male staff and female passengers. To have to smile and wait on a new group of passengers week after week seemed to me to be a phony existence.

Despite my awareness of the psychopathology aboard the cruise ship, I found Rachel different. She didn't seem to be artificial. She seemed to be very genuine. Her life story was full of tragedy, but you had to pull it out of her. I detected nothing in her behavior that even suggested psychopathology. She appeared normal, and her behavior seemed to be consistent with that of a female brought up in South America.

I questioned Rachel about why she was on the ship and had left her sons at home. She said she missed her sons terribly, but she did this for them. She felt they needed to gain independence from her.

RELATIONSHIP WITH RACHEL

This was something she did as a sacrifice for her children. She showed me pictures of her sons. The widow's pension she received from the Spanish government was directly placed in a joint account she had established with her children, and they drew on this money to live. The money she earned on board the ship was used to pay off the mortgage and assist her children if necessary. Because everything about her appeared to be so unselfish, I accepted this explanation. Rachel was very convincing. I was responding to the person not the facts.

Only after the relationship ended did I realize that a normal mother, especially someone from a Spanish background, would never behave in this way. Mothers do not leave home to enable their children to gain independence! Especially when their children are still in school. I wanted to believe, so I did. What I saw as unselfish was actually narcissistic. It would be easy to dismiss this false perception on my part with the statement that there is no fool like an old fool or love is blind. But I do not think that applies. Rachel's mask was very good; she was very convincing. Based on my own experience with my mother, I believed a mother could be as unselfish and masochistic as Rachel portrayed herself. Her behavior on board the ship was consistent with this image.

When I left the ship to return to the United States, I told her I would call her in Spain. I called as promised. She repeated her invitation to come to

Spain. I didn't know what to expect, so I planned a trip of three weeks, thinking I would spend a few days with her and the rest of the time traveling around Spain.

SPAIN, NOVEMBER 1991

When I arrived at her home (in a resort area to the north of Barcelona), I had no idea of the living arrangements. We hadn't even kissed up to this point. I met her sons and they appeared well-adjusted. I was keenly interested in her sons, how they would view me, and what effects their father's suicide had on them. I sensed no problems.

The house was small, with four bedrooms, furnished modestly with old furniture. It appeared to lack a woman's touch. I do not recall seeing family pictures around the house. No picture of Georgio was visible. The house lacked warmth; it was more like a dormitory for her sons.

Rachel had bought a new revealing nightgown for my visit. We slept together the first night, and our love making was tender and giving on both sides. She was uninhibited sexually and eagerly satisfied my every desire. This continued almost up to the very end of our relationship.

During my stay at her home, I remember two incidents vividly.

One incident involved my playfully waving my

RELATIONSHIP WITH RACHEL

hand back and forth in front of her face as if I were slapping her. I do not recall why it was done, but I was just innocently teasing her and acting with affection. (I didn't touch her.) She reacted with explosive anger that caused me to jump back. "Don't ever do that again," she said; indicating that her mother used to beat her and this reawakened those memories. Despite her mother's beatings, Rachel reported standing her ground and resisting her mother. Rachel would not yield. This story in some ways characterized Rachel's personality. On one hand she was dependent, servile, unselfish, amiable, and compassionate; on the other hand she was stubborn, independent, narcissistic, and ruthless.

The other incident occurred on the second morning of my visit. Rachel asked if she could shave me. She used to shave her father, she said. No one had ever shaved me, nor had it ever crossed my mind for a woman to do this. Frankly, I can do a better job myself; but it is nice being pampered. Since that time I have asked other American men if their wives ever shaved them. The answer has always been in the negative. When I have asked American wives if they have ever shaved their husbands, I generally do not receive a direct answer but rather a look of incredulousness and laughter. Actually, women in South America and Spanish speaking countries often do shave their husbands or fathers.

We spent the next few days at her home. She

never seemed to want to go anywhere. She was adverse to traveling to Barcelona because of the traffic. She just seemed to want to stay around the house, and I became restless. One day she relented and took me sightseeing. We then decided to travel around Spain together. I think we both enjoyed ourselves, and she visited places she had never seen. On this trip around Spain we had one fight, and she stormed out of the place where we were eating. The fight involved my asking some questions about her finances. I had to pull the information out of her. She would tell me one thing; and then I would ask another question, and she would tell me something different. Apart from that one incident, we enjoyed being with one another.

While we were in Madrid (in late November 1991), she faxed a letter to the Olympus Cruise office in Greece stating she would not be a social hostess on the Piraeus that winter because she had never received a signed contract. The fax went out just days before she was to join the ship. She had decided to spend the winter with me.

When we returned to her house, she told her sons we were married. They looked at her with disbelief. "You went through a marriage ceremony?" her oldest son asked. She said that we had not, but we considered ourselves to be married.

If I had not found Rachel on board the ship already separated from her sons, I would never have taken her from her sons to the United States. I saw the relationship as being a positive one for her boys. They were entering manhood, and I could serve as a mentor and avuncular figure. I could bring stability to the family. They were all alone in Spain without any family. I had extensive family in the United States and could offer them roots and facilitate employment opportunities. I saw our relationship as being beneficial to Rachel as well as her sons. I had reached a stage in life where giving rather than building was important.

At the end of the three weeks in Spain, we decided to travel to the United States and spend the winter in Mexico and South America. This was my idea. I had intended to do this prior to meeting Rachel. Rachel merely made the trip easier for me since Spanish was her native language. We viewed our arrangements as a non-legal marriage. I recognized that we knew one another an insufficient time to make a life-time commitment and told her if things did not work out, I would pay for her travel arrangements back to Spain.

BOSTON, DECEMBER 1991

The first few weeks in the United States were spent in a suburb outside of Boston where I had an apartment. Rachel proved to have excellent domestic skills. She was a creative cook, good at housecleaning, unbelievable in sewing skills, highly developed in

RACHEL'S BURNING BUSH

mechanical skills, a skillful auto driver, and a natural hostess. She was a hard-working woman, capable in her own right, upbeat and happy, friendly with others, demure and feminine. She was solicitous toward me as well as toward my friends. She was happy making me happy. I spent the weeks in Boston preparing for our extensive trip to South America. We were going to spend three weeks in Mexico, one week in Venezuela, one week at Margarita Island off the coast of Venezuela, one week in Brazil, a week at Iguacu Falls, one week in Argentina, three weeks in Chile, one week in Ecuador, one week at the Galapagos Islands, and one week in the Amazon. We would be traveling as independent travelers without prearranged tours.

A number of events stand out in my mind during these first few weeks in Boston.

As I recall one of the first things we did when we came to Boston was to visit my parents' graves. It was important for me to present Rachel to them. Either at this time or later, Rachel indicated she wanted to spend not only this life with me but also all eternity and be buried with me in Boston. That is a really strong statement to make so early in a relationship. She referred to me as her "burning bush." I did not accept this literally to mean God, but as a metaphor to mean someone special whom you admire. Spanish speaking people often use flowery expressions, and I accepted Rachel's "burning bush" comment in that light. People remarked that they had never met a woman who appeared to be so much in love. It was almost unreal. She treated me like I was her gift from heaven.

It used to be a family practice to have a Friday-evening meal together to welcome in the Sabbath. My mother would light the Sabbath candles, we would say the Kiddush (the blessing for the wine) and the blessing for the bread. It was a time of peace and camaraderie. An invited guest made it even more joyous. When my mother died, this practice lapsed. My youngest brother, Esteban, who lived in Boston was also a bachelor. We went out to dinner together on Friday night, but it was not the same.

Rachel changed all this. She lit the candles on Friday night. I invited my brother over for Friday-night dinner. The family was together again. I invited some cousins and friends to join us. My cup runneth over with pleasure. My brother silently noted my pleasure. For the first time in my life, I appeared happy. Rachel had made a home for me. Our home.

My female friends and family were uncomfortable with Rachel. They didn't understand her. It didn't make sense to them that a mother would leave sons at home and go away with a man to another country.

They also saw her as too good, too solicitous, too giving, too obsequious. She would not accept help from anyone. If I would ask her something or ask her to do something, she would jump or run to comply. They tried to persuade her to act otherwise.

I told them to leave her alone. I felt that what we were seeing was a cultural difference. While we in the United States were caught up in the equality of women, women of Rachel's age in South America and in other parts of the world were still operating from the position that women took care of the house, and men were responsible for protecting and taking care of women. I felt that if this behavior was natural for Rachel, then it was okay with me, for I knew something that none of the others knew. This wasn't a one-way street. Rachel received from me love, admiration, respect, a desire and commitment to make her happy and to take care of her. Ours was a relationship involving not selfishness but giving and making the other party happy.

Another event also stands out. We used to go walking in the morning. One morning we went walking at a local high-school running track. The conversation was light and we were enjoying ourselves. Suddenly, Rachel turned around and began walking in the other direction around the track. I continued walking and we met walking in opposite directions. I told her I was leaving and going home, but she continued to walk around the track. I left the track and headed home. Every few hundred yards, I would turn around to see if she was following. I didn't understand what was going on. Rachel not only did not know the way home, but she didn't even know the address. When I reached home, I drove back to the track. Rachel was sitting on a rock outside the track like a little girl waiting to be picked up. She didn't say anything; she just got in the car as if nothing happened. She wasn't upset. This was really strange behavior and more than miscommunication, more than a game or prank she was playing. But it was an isolated event, not part of a trend, and I chose not to make a big deal out of it.

One of Rachel's sons, Jacob, who was studying in France, came to the United States to visit with his girl friend. I suggested they stay at my condo in Florida for a week and enjoy themselves. We would be down in a week and try to rent out the condo for the period we would be traveling in South America. Jacob accepted my invitation.

MY BROTHER'S DEATH

Rachel and I packed our things and started to drive to Florida. Our intent was to first stop off at her sister's house in northern Virginia and then at my brother Julio's new vacation house in southern Virginia. We reached her sister's house by mid-afternoon. A few hours later I received a call from Esteban. (He had to call Rachel's home in Spain to obtain Leah's number.) The minute I heard his voice, I knew what had happened. My brother Julio had died. Julio had a heart attack the year after I had my first attack. I was just a hundred miles from his vacation home. I was looking forward with some excitement to visiting with him, my nieces, and my sister-in-law.

Julio's home was in Albany, New York, but he had a family burial plot in Boston. I discussed with Rachel the options available to her. She could stay with her sister for the week I was back North, or she could come with me. I encouraged her to stay with her sister and use this time to cement family ties. She wanted to go with me and felt her place was with me. We first drove to Boston and attended the funeral. In the Jewish religion there is a week of mourning called the week of Shiva. The first few days of Shiva were spent in Boston at Esteban's home. We then drove to Albany and spent the remaining part of the week of Shiva at Julio's home. I think of my brother often and visit his grave three or four times a year.

Rachel was very helpful to the family during these trying times. With the death of my mother and the death of my brother, the relationship with Rachel provided support and foundation in my life. I did not need her in some neurotic sense; but she was very supportive, and I appreciated her support.

We drove back from Albany to Boston at the end of the week of Shiva. I had mixed feelings about going to South America but decided it would be best to travel and keep busy. We drove back to Virginia and stayed at her sister's place for the night. Her sister felt we were using her house as a motel, and I decided that in the future we would not stay there.

FLORIDA, JANUARY 1992

When we arrived at my Florida condo, I found it untidy. Dishes were in the sink, writing paper was scattered around the living room, and the bedroom was in a state of disarray—with the beds unmade and clothes and luggage scattered around the room. I was annoyed. I explained to her son, Jacob, that I had come here to rent out the condo and the place had to be kept clean and neat because I would be showing the place to prospective tenants. I also told him that he couldn't leave dishes in the sink. I was firm and heavy handed. The condo association had rules as to where guests could park their cars and what hours the pool could be used. I advised Jacob of these details. Jacob, and the two girls he was with, just wanted to enjoy themselves and felt intimidated by me and my demands.

The night before they were leaving, they decided to have their dinner on the lanai. Rachel told me to stay away from them; they wanted to be alone. They thought I was "worse than military." They were afraid of me and didn't like me. I was to stay away from the lanai and not upset them.

I listened to Rachel in disbelief. This was my

condo. I was being told by my guests to stay away from them, and that my lanai was off limits to me. Rachel did not tell me this with a sense of compassion or kindness, but rather it was said to me with anger and enmity. She was in complete sympathy with her son's demands. (Much later Jacob told me that he had been joking, and they had a pleasant time and fond memories of their stay.)

I became really angry. I couldn't believe what I had heard. They were taking over my condo and telling me what I was to do! I felt like going in to them and telling them to leave the condo: pack their bags, leave, and take Rachel with them. But I decided to cool it. I left the condo and stayed at Esteban's condo nearby.

I returned early the next morning. Rachel said she had been up all night. I didn't speak with her and went out for a morning walk. When I returned, Jacob had left. There was tenseness in the air for a few hours, but things quieted down and we resumed our relationship. I was puzzled by Rachel's behavior. As a social hostess, she knew how to handle people. Assuming that Jacob's feelings were as stated, Rachel could have suggested we go out for dinner rather than provoking a confrontation. In retrospect the feelings Rachel projected onto Jacob were actually her own. I didn't understand this at the time because she behaved in such an opposite mode toward me most of the time.

We remained in Florida a week and then flew to

RELATIONSHIP WITH RACHEL

the Yucatan Peninsula of Mexico.

For the next three weeks we traveled throughout Mexico and then spent two months visiting South America. This period was like an extended honeymoon. We bonded as a couple, enjoyed one another's company, laughed, made love, delighted in the sights, and experienced the native populations. Other than having two fights, we got along well.

Rachel was so involved with me that I would be the one, more often than not, to remind her to call her sons in Spain. Her devotion and love for me was so complete that everything else was pushed aside.

While Rachel and I did not fight, there were almost daily tête-à-têtes between local vendors and me. These confrontations frequently were both acerbic and vociferous. They almost always involved monetary fights with hotel personnel, taxi vendors, or travel agents. The battles were never ending and unquestionably were the major source of aggravation on our trip. This impacted on our relationship.

In writing about our journey, I have focused on problems rather than the good times. And there were many good times. But since this relationship ultimately ended, the problems serve to shed some light on the underlying tension that existed.

MEXICO

I had made arrangements through a travel agency

RACHEL'S BURNING BUSH

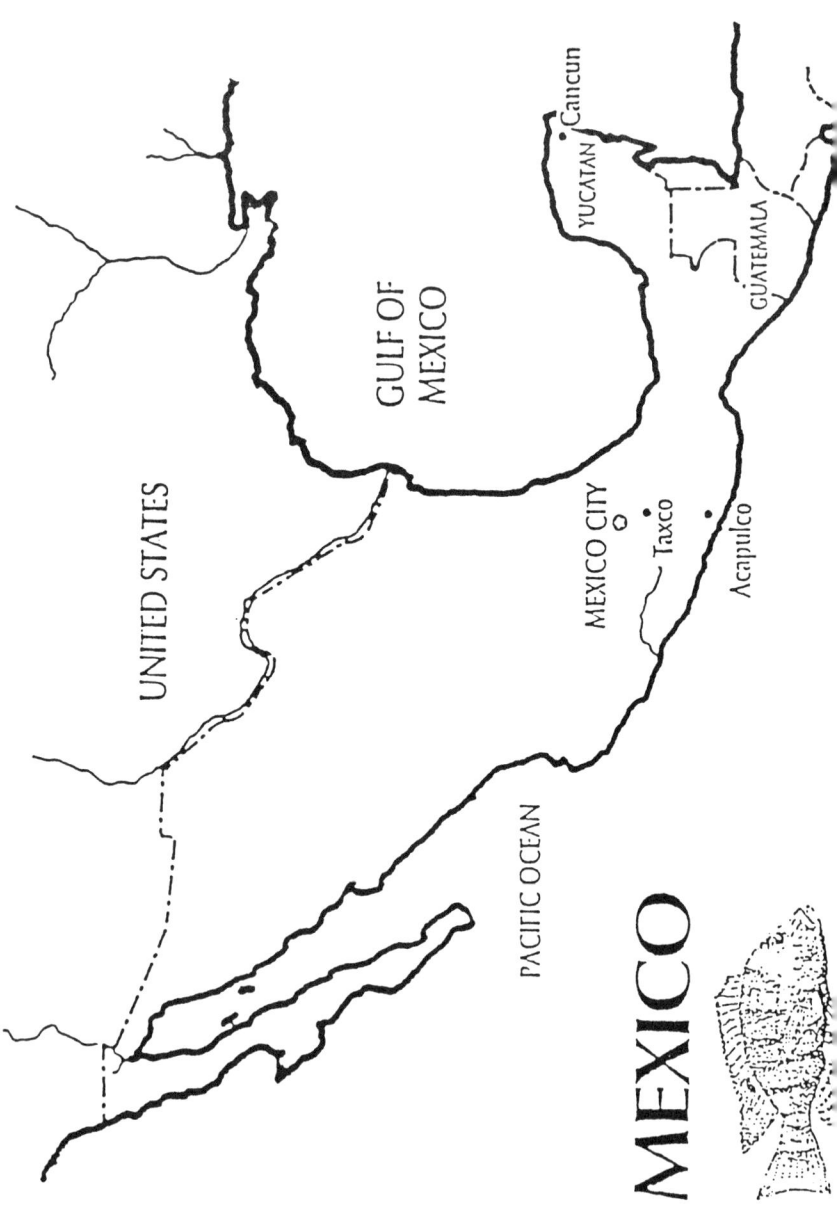

RELATIONSHIP WITH RACHEL

for reservations at a Best Western Motel in Cancun. After the first day, I noticed in my AAA travel book that rooms at the motel were listed at ten dollars less per night than we were being charged. I approached the management with the book and my AAA membership card and wanted to know if an adjustment could be made on the remaining nights we were to stay. I agreed to pay the higher rate for the first night but wanted the lower rate for the rest of our stay.

The management initially rejected my request. Rachel sided with the management and felt I was wrong. She took the position that I had made a reservation at the higher rate and should keep to my agreement. I pointed out to her that our reservation was for one night only, this was a daily not a weekly rate we were paying, and we were free to leave at any time. She stuck to her position. This was the first of many disagreements we had over money matters. Throughout our trip she frequently sided with the other party when there were monetary disputes. I never understood this, and this became a point of divisiveness between us. To me her position represented a lack of loyalty, bonding and identification with us as a couple. It was my money not our money. This was inconsistent with planning to spend a life with someone.

I should have recognized that this behavior, which was to repeat itself again and again, was a sign of ambivalence which ultimately would lead to the denouement of our relationship.

The motel subsequently agreed to lower the rate by ten dollars as I had requested.

Rachel just wanted to enjoy the trip, and she felt I was approaching everything like a business decision. She was right. I was unable to discard years of carefully monitoring money matters. I was unable to change my ways. It wasn't that I was cheap, and wouldn't spend money—I ended up spending over thirty-three thousand dollars on this trip and close to twenty thousand dollars on my European trip just months before—but I do not like to feel that I have been taken advantage of. During this trip we stayed for the most part at five-star hotels. Quality, not luxury, is important to me, and it became evident as the trip progressed that it was necessary to stay at the best hotels to ensure quality even if this meant paying two hundred dollars or more a night.

I have subsequently learned to travel to foreign countries with a different mind set. The wages for the average person in many foreign countries is much lower than it is in the United States. I am viewed as a wealthy American, and it is accepted practice to overcharge and defraud. It is not worth fighting all the time. Ten dollars, one hundred dollars, even five hundred dollars is not going to break me. I have learned to accept the inevitable and enjoy my travel.

We drove around the Yucatan. The highlights were the Mayan ruins at Uxmal and the pyramids of

RELATIONSHIP WITH RACHEL

Chichén-itzá. I recall Rachel climbing the pyramids to the top while I remained below. She was like a small child going up on all fours.

We then flew to Mexico City. I had problems breathing in the city because of the altitude of seventy-five hundred feet and pollution in the air. We stayed at a hotel facing the zocalo or square. On the second night I developed Montezuma's revenge and was quite ill for a day. I woke up in the middle of the night vomiting and with diarrhea. It was a mess. I was embarrassed but too ill to do anything about it. Rachel behaved in a caring and loving manner. She cleaned up the mess, washed my soiled clothes, and took care of me. After a day in bed, I was fine. We continued to see the sights around Mexico City. We made a side trip to the Aztec Pyramids and Temples at Teotihuacan.

One day we planned to visit the American Embassy and extend Rachel's visa from ninety days to six months. In the afternoon before we were to visit the embassy, a taxi driver offered to drive us the next morning at 9:00 A.M. We accepted and told him to be on time. The next day we were ready to go at 8:50 A.M., and I hailed a taxi to take us. Rachel insisted we wait for the other taxi driver. We had a commitment to him she maintained. I told her that was nonsense. He was cruising the city; if he picked up another fare, he would take it. We should "flag" a taxi while we could. She was adamant; and so we waited.

RACHEL'S BURNING BUSH

At 9:15 A.M. he still had not arrived. We could not find another taxi and were forced to take a private hotel taxi to the embassy. It cost me an extra ten to fifteen dollars for this unmetered taxi. I was angry at her for causing me this unnecessary expense and delay. That night Rachel told me she wanted to end the trip and return home. She just didn't want any more fights. She had made a mistake in coming with me. I was not the same man she had met on the cruise ship. After some talking, we made up and continued on our trip. In some ways this was a repeat of what happened in Cancun. A small amount of money was involved but came to represent a schism between us—Rachel siding with the local people, while I was looking out for my interests. This pattern would continue throughout our trip!

We then drove to Acapulco for a week of rest and relaxation.

Before returning to Mexico City we stopped in Taxco, which is known as the silver city. We arrived during the early evening. On the outskirts of the town, a man approached us. He told us he was from the tourist office and would help us locate a motel—there was no charge for his service. We followed him to a nearby official-looking house, and he arranged to obtain a room for us at a motel. When we arrived at the motel, the hotel clerk advised us the room would be much higher than we had been quoted and what was listed in our tourist books. He told us he had to pay the booking agent commissions for all tourists sent to him. We advised him we came on our own and received the reduced room rate. That evening we ate in the motel dining room.

When we checked out the next morning, we found our bill higher than expected. The charge for the dinner meal was thirty dollars higher than listed on the menu from which we had ordered. I asked to see the menu. They produced a menu with the higher price, but it wasn't the same menu from which we had ordered. I didn't know what was going on. Finally, by chance, I turned the menu over. Eureka! The backside was the menu from which we had ordered. The higher-priced menu with a more complete selection of food was the dinner menu and had the heading Comida. The menu we were given was the luncheon menu with a more limited selection of food, a lower tariff and had the heading Almuerzo which means lunch. At the time I didn't know much Spanish. Almuerzo and Comida didn't mean anything to me. I relied on Rachel to translate for me. She had said nothing. She joined me however in arguing with the people to give us the reduced rate. They finally complied with our request. To this day I am not sure if Rachel's behavior reflected incompetence on her part, lack of worldly sophistication, female passivity and dependence on the male to make decisions, or a more sinister motive to harm me.

Later in the day we toured Taxco. I bought her

an expensive silver-pearl necklace and some other jewelry.

We then drove back to Mexico City and flew to Caracas, Venezuela. Again we had problems.

VENEZUELA

From the Caracas Airport, we took a taxi to our hotel. During our stay the bathroom was always flooded either from an overflow from the shower or from around the base of the toilet. Despite sending up a plumber, the problem continued. To add insult to injury, when we checked out of the hotel we found they charged us fifteen dollars extra per night above the price they had quoted us for the room. They claimed it was a larger room than what they had quoted. I asked for the manager, but was told he would not be back until the afternoon. I just paid the bill by credit card and when I returned to the United States explained the situation to the credit-card company and received credit for the overcharge.

We went to an American Express travel-agency affiliate in Caracas to arrange for a trip to Margarita Island off the coast of Venezuela. The people at the agency did not speak English very well and communication was a problem. Once again Rachel was of minimal help. It appeared to me that she lacked the intellect to deal with the myriad details of arranging a

RELATIONSHIP WITH RACHEL

RACHEL'S BURNING BUSH

trip. Even on the simplest trip there are all sorts of options and interconnections that must be considered. Finally the trip was arranged. The tickets and travel plans were in Spanish. I misunderstood the verbal instructions and misread the Spanish directions. The end result was that we missed our plane and had to make a later flight to Margarita Island. We had arranged to have a private car from the travel agency pick us up. Since we were late, our prearranged pick up had come and gone. We were told to take a local taxi to our motel. The taxi charge was around five dollars. We had paid the American Express travel agency around thirty dollars for the same trip. We told them to forget about picking us up and returning us to the airport. Rachel expressed some guilt at not at least looking at the tickets and instructions and advising me of the correct times.

One thing that stands out in my mind about Venezuela (and for most of South America for that matter) was the police. They all wore bullet-proof vests and carried sub-machine guns. They all appeared very young. At my request Rachel asked one of them why they were attired this way. We were told: "Don't ask. We shoot first, and ask questions later." At that response Rachel grabbed me and pulled me away. Throughout our journey in South America, I saw the fear people had of the police and heard stories about people being taken to prison and never heard from again. The day after we left Venezuela, we heard there had been an unsuccessful military coup d' état.

BRAZIL

We flew from Caracas to Rio de Janeiro in Brazil.

We opted to stay in a five-star two hundred dollar a night hotel in the Copacabana Beach area. The hotel had all the trappings of a once great hotel in a state of decline. The furnishings in the room were on par with a run-down hotel in the United States priced in the twenty to thirty dollar range. All the water in the bathroom was brown in color including the water from the shower, from the sink, and in the toilet. I couldn't believe it, for over two hundred dollars a day! Apparently the water in Rio de Janeiro at that time was brown colored.

We decided to change our plans. Rather than stay in Rio, we thought it would be best to go directly to Iguacu Falls which is on the border between Brazil and Argentina. I went over to a local office of Varig Airlines, the Brazilian owned and operated airline, which owns a hotel bordering the falls. I thought it would be romantic to stay right on the falls. The young woman who arranged our flight also arranged our room reservations at the hotel. She claimed the price would be around one hundred twenty dollars per night if we paid cash now or about two hundred dollars per night if we paid by credit card at the hotel.

RACHEL'S BURNING BUSH

She could not guarantee us a reservation unless we paid in cash. I didn't want to chance flying to the falls and not be able to find a room so I paid her in cash. When we arrived at the hotel at the falls, we realized once again we had been taken. The room rate was the same whether you paid by cash or credit card—around one hundred twenty dollars a night. There were plenty of rooms available since this was the off season.

IGUACU FALLS

We visited Iguacu Falls on a glorious sunny day. This was probably the highlight of our trip. The falls were magnificent and more breathtaking than Niagara Falls. Iguacu just went on and on. It was enormous. We walked right up to the falls and felt the water spraying on us, and then we walked into a cave situated just within the falls and experienced the majesty and thunderous power of the roaring water. After dinner we strolled to the falls and enjoyed the ambience from a moonlit night.

We also took a day to visit the Indian markets in Paraguay.

From Iguacu Falls we flew to Buenos Aires, Argentina.

ARGENTINA

I knew the taxi ride from the airport to down-

RELATIONSHIP WITH RACHEL

town Buenos Aires would be expensive. Before entering the taxi, I was quoted a price of forty-six dollars. When we arrived at our five-star hotel, I went in to check on our reservation which supposedly had been made by Varig Airlines. The female clerk at Varig not only had deceived me with the cash versus credit-card routine, but she had lied to me about making reservations at the hotel. The hotel did not have a reservation for us, but there were plenty of rooms so there was no problem. About four to five minutes later, I emerged from the hotel to take our bags from the taxi and pay the driver. The fare was now fifty-eight dollars, not forty-six dollars. I made a comment to Rachel about being ripped off again. Rachel disagreed. The twelve dollars surcharge made sense to her—I had kept the man waiting outside for five minutes.

The month of February is the summer season in Argentina, and the temperature was over ninety degrees. For some reason the air conditioning system was not working properly throughout the hotel. When we returned from dinner and went up to our room, I experienced breathing problems. They tried to help: they brought in fans; they sent up an engineer to work on our air conditioning system; they changed our room in the hope that this would help. Nothing helped. I was gasping for air. Finally I made a decision to find another hotel with air conditioning. This five-star hotel was costing me over two hundred dollars a night.

RACHEL'S BURNING BUSH

I found a three-star hotel with breakfast and with air conditioning for seventy dollars a night. We took a taxi from one hotel to the other hotel.

The taxi ride was less than two blocks and took only a few minutes. When we arrived at the second hotel, I asked Rachel to find out what the fare was. She told me twenty dollars. I said, "Rachel, you have to be joking—twenty dollars for a two-minute ride?" I went into the hotel and asked the clerk what it should cost by taxi for such a ride. He told me two dollars and accompanied me to the taxi and spoke with the driver. The driver agreed on the two dollar fare. I asked Rachel what was wrong with her? How could she tell me twenty dollars? She told me that was what the driver said. The words in Spanish are "dos" for two and "veinte" for twenty. They do not sound alike, and there was no way she could mistake the two words. But "Rachel," I said, "where is your head? Twenty dollars for a ride around the block?" She answered: "It cost fifty-eight dollars from the airport (an hour's ride), I figured twenty dollars was reasonable." I just shook my head in disbelief. To this day I do not know whether she was an unsophisticated child or she had some macabre hidden motive and agenda. It didn't make sense to me that a person who had traveled so widely and lived in so many countries could be so naive.

One incident that upset Rachel occurred at the office of American Airlines. We had been busy

RELATIONSHIP WITH RACHEL

throughout the day and arrived at the airline office at 5:00 P.M. Just as we approached the front door, the guard closed it and would not let us in. I tried to speak with him, but he couldn't understand English. He just waved us away. In my frustration I kicked the door and banged it with my fist a couple of times. This outburst of anger upset Rachel. There was a lot of frustration I was experiencing in not being able to communicate and understand the customs. Some businesses closed in the afternoon and remained open in the evening; other businesses remained open in the afternoon and closed at 5:00 P.M.

Repeatedly in our stay in Buenos Aires we were subject to overcharging by taxi drivers. Without question Argentina had the worst taxi bandits of any country I have ever visited. In every country I have been in, including the United States, taxi drivers defraud their customers. But Buenos Aires was something special! It was so egregious that it curtailed our stay in the country.

Buenos Aires has a famous shopping street called Florida. Leather goods and sweaters are well known products from this country. I bought Rachel a number of beautiful and very expensive sweaters as well as a leather belt. We then went to a cafeteria-style vegetarian restaurant. When we were seated, I asked Rachel to find out what the costs of our meals would be. She left the table and came back and told me the price was fifty dollars. That seemed very high to me, so I went and spoke to the cashier/manager who told me the price was five dollars. This time I didn't make a big deal of it.

We hired a taxi to take us to the Buenos Aires airport for our flight to Chile. I was very careful this time. I had the hotel manager accompany me to the taxi, and he and the driver agreed on a flat fee of thirty-eight dollars, no extras for bags, bridges, or traffic problems. When we arrived at the airport, I gave the driver a fifty-dollar bill, and he gave me seven dollars back. I told him he owed me another five dollars. He insisted seven dollars was the correct change and hastily drove off. Rachel just stood on the sidewalk and said nothing. She stated she had to remain with our bags or they would have been stolen.

Rachel reminded me that this was South America not the United States. I was expecting things to be like the United States, and that is not the way things were in South America. While she was from Chile, she appeared to identify with South America and appeared to take my complaints about being ripped off on a personal basis—that these were her people with whom I was finding fault. I think in part that is why she was siding with those people who were involved in shams against me. She was identifying more with the working people who short changed me than she was with me. On the other hand, every other aspect of her behavior appeared to reflect a sense of togetherness with me, kindness toward me, love, happiness, joy—a real commitment to the relationship coupled with an effort to make me happy.

While Rachel seemed to be cavalier about the money I spent, she was penurious about the spending money that I had given her or her own money. Rachel never asked me for anything and never indicated she would like anything which involved the spending of any money. She just seemed to want nothing to do with the details of the trip and the monetary transactions. I recall an incident when she was considering buying some costume jewelry from a sidewalk vendor. The man wanted two dollars for a ring, and Rachel only wanted to spend one dollar of her money. She really wanted the ring, but she would not spend the extra dollar. Her behavior puzzled me.

CHILE

We flew into Santiago, Chile from Buenos Aires. As we crossed from one country to the other the beautiful Andes Mountains were in our view. Rachel pointed this out to me with national pride. After landing at the Santiago airport, we took a special bus into the city and then hailed a cab to the Holiday Inn where we had our reservation. From my reading of the various travel guides, I knew the taxi fares in Santiago were reasonably priced. The ride to the hotel was ten blocks and took about seven minutes. I asked Rachel to find out from the driver how much the fare was. She told me thirty-nine hundred seventy pesos which was somewhere between ten and twelve dollars at the exchange rate. I told her that was too high, the man was ripping us off. She responded by saying that the meter started at zero, the meter said thirty-nine hundred seventy and the driver said thirty-nine hundred seventy. I paid the driver the fare.

When we went into the hotel, I asked the concierge what the taxi charge was from the bus station to the hotel. He told me five hundred pesos (one dollar fifty cents) at most. I became very angry at Rachel. This was her country; she had lived in Santiago; she had been to the city in 1987; she knew what things cost. I told her she was part of the mafia trying to rip me off. Instead of trying to protect me, instead of looking out for my welfare, she was in collusion with others intent on defrauding me. I was just venting frustration and certainly did not think she was in collusion with or part of the mafia. It was just cumulative frustration building up inside of me. I did not speak or understand Spanish, and I was relying on her to translate and protect my/our interests. She reacted to my charge with anger and told me she wanted to go home. She couldn't take it any more from me. By the next day we had cooled down and things returned to normal.

The first day in Santiago we walked around the city seeing the sights. She also contacted her in-laws and arranged to visit them the next day. They lived in

RELATIONSHIP WITH RACHEL

a residential area of Santiago. She went there the first thing in the morning, and I continued sightseeing on my own. I received a phone call from Rachel indicating they would like to meet me. Her father-in-law picked me up at the hotel, and we had lunch at the family home. I met Rachel's mother-in-law and brother-in-law at the home. They were friendly people and treated Rachel like a daughter. When we left, Rachel's mother-in-law placed a diamond ring in Rachel's hand as a going away present and as a token of love and affection. That evening we had dinner at Rachel's brother-in-law's house where I met Rachel's sister-in-law. The couple were both professional people, and I enjoyed the evening's conversation. They treated Rachel like family.

The next few days we spent around Santiago. We spent one morning visiting the grave of one of her parents. I do not remember the cemetery very clearly. The grave was in poor condition, and Rachel obtained the name of the caretaker and promised to send her some money with instructions on maintaining the grave. I do not remember whether this was the grave of her father or mother. I do remember standing with Rachel by the grave and silently saying I would take care of Rachel and that her parent could rest in peace. When we left the cemetery, Rachel pointed to another cemetery where Georgio (her husband) was buried. I asked if she wanted to visit the grave—it would be all right with me—but she declined saying she was with me, and she was my wife now.

Most of the time however was spent arranging travel for the next leg of our trip. We went to a travel agency located next to the Holiday Inn that had been recommended by the hotel staff. I wanted to arrange a trip to the Galapagos Islands. The people at the agency did not speak English very well. They said they could arrange the trip but would need a deposit of three hundred dollars in cash to cover out-of-pocket expenses for phone calls and faxes to Ecuador. I asked them if the three hundred dollars would be returned if they could not make reservations on the dates we specified. They answered in the affirmative. I gave them the money somewhat reluctantly, but I thought I was safe since the agency was located within the Holiday Inn plaza. Rachel excused herself and went upstairs to our room. She just didn't seem to be interested in the myriad details. This later proved to be a mistake.

After numerous delays in finalizing the arrangement, the agency contacted us and told me to come down for our tickets. I owed another twenty-six hundred dollars for the package tour. I gave them a credit card; but they said they didn't accept credit cards for this tour, and I had to pay cash. I told them I couldn't and wouldn't pay them twenty-six hundred dollars in cash and asked for my deposit of three hundred dollars back. They replied they couldn't do this; the three hundred dollars was for administrative expenses and was non refundable. I hit the roof! I started screaming and yelling like a mad man. Everyone in the office was rooted in fear. I left the travel-agency office in a state of fury, first stopping in our room to tell Rachel what had happened (screaming at her that I had been ripped off again but this time for three hundred dollars), and then went up to see the manager of the hotel.

I came into his office and requested that he call the police. He asked me what had happened and after hearing the story called the travel agency. The agency, despite his threat not to send any more hotel customers, would not return the three hundred dollars. He turned to me and said he could do nothing, and I should be more careful. Shortly thereafter Rachel appeared at the door. In a little girl voice she said, "Hello," and sat down shyly next to me. As she handed me three hundred dollars she asked, "Is this what you were looking for?" We both looked at her in amazement. "How did you get the three hundred dollars?" we asked. She said when she went into the travel agency some of the people were in tears, and the man I dealt with was so upset he had to go home. I had really scared them. She spoke with the female owner who had returned to the office after I left and asked her how many pesos she had on her person. The woman answered about four thousand pesos. "The two thousand six hundred dollars was close to a million pesos," Rachel stated. "If you are carrying only four

RACHEL'S BURNING BUSH

thousand pesos on your person, how would you expect us to carry over a million pesos? If you traveled, would you expect to pay for this with a credit card or cash?" The woman claimed she had paid the three hundred dollars to a master travel agent who covered the Galapagos Islands for all of Chile, and this agent would not return the three hundred dollars to her. Somehow or other Rachel manipulated the woman to giving back the three hundred dollars. I was not surprised. Rachel was a master at manipulating people. She remained cool under fire and pressed her point until the other side gave in. I felt, however, like many of the problems I ran into, this confrontation could have been avoided if Rachel had played a more active and protective role in the beginning. This was her country, she spoke Spanish, the people at the agency spoke English poorly. If they had conversed in Spanish, this misunderstanding might never have occurred.

    We rented a car from Avis which had a rental office in the lobby of the Holiday Inn. Rachel again remained in the background as I tried to work out the details with the female clerk who spoke English poorly. The Avis forms were in Spanish, and I had to ask for detailed explanations for what I was signing. Because of all the problems I experienced on this trip, I was extra careful and went over the forms in great detail.

    We decided to drive south to visit the town of Concepcion where Rachel grew up and then on to

RELATIONSHIP WITH RACHEL

Puerto Montt and the Glaciers in southern Chile. Concepcion is a small town. Here, a small group of Jews, fleeing from Europe both before and after the Second World War, settled and raised their families. They built a small synagogue. Within a larger gentile cemetery, they had made a small Jewish section. Within minutes of our arriving in Concepcion, Rachel met close family friends walking in the center of town: two brothers—I assume contemporaries of Rachel's parents—and their wives. They were in the lumber business (Chile is a large exporter of lumber) and held large reserves of lumber. Rachel referred to one of the these gentlemen as her first "burning bush." It was a real compliment. This man was courtly, distinguished, very wealthy, a leading and respected citizen of the town.

The hotels in town were full, and we stayed at the home of an anthropology professor and his wife who was from Germany. I had a delightful time here. Each morning we had breakfast with the couple and enjoyed a lively discussion. Actually it was the professor, his wife and I who did most of the talking. Rachel was quiet as usual. In fact, at no time did I ever hear Rachel engage in active conversation when we were with a group of people. Her conversation style was to ask a leading question and then let people talk. This passivity existed even when she was with Spanish-speaking people. This appeared to be more from a lack of education than from shyness.

RACHEL'S BURNING BUSH

In Concepcion we visited the two homes in which Rachel had lived. They were small but adequate homes. One of them had been converted into the leading restaurant in town. We visited the cemetery where Rachel's other parent was buried. Again I stood with Rachel by the grave and silently spoke my vow to take care of her; her parent could rest in peace. We also visited the synagogue and stood before the Ark together and said vows silently. The Ark has special meaning and is considered a holy place within the synagogue. To stand together as a couple before the Ark is not to be taken lightly. It is like standing before God.

I had an opportunity to meet many members of the small Jewish community in Concepcion. Without exception, they welcomed Rachel with open arms. Like Georgio's family in Santiago, the Jewish community in Concepcion were exceptionally warm toward her.

We went to a travel agency in Concepcion owned by a friend of Rachel's sister. The owner welcomed Rachel with great warmth. We explained that we wanted to go to the Galapagos Islands in Ecuador, the Amazon in Brazil, and the Glaciers in southern Chile. We would not pay by cash, only by credit card. We would not pay anything up front until the reservations were confirmed and tickets issued. He indicated the trip to the Glaciers was by cash. He had to pay the Patagonia—the name of the company as well as the name of the cruise ship to the Glaciers—in cash. They gave him a commission for the sale. He could invoice the credit-card company for the total amount of the trip, but they would take a four-percent discount when they paid him. If we agreed to a four-percent premium on the credit card, he would handle it that way. In this way we could conserve our cash. The trip to the Galapagos Islands and Amazon were arranged according to the same scheme. The one exception was the plane fare to the Galapagos Islands which would be issued by an associate travel agency in Ecuador. We would pay them by credit card when we arrived there. Everything else was taken care of. Again, Rachel was only partially involved—more than before, but she was not able to handle the details. The trip required careful scheduling of planes, boat trips, hotels, car rentals, driving distances, the beginning and ending days for each tour, and sights to visit. I do not feel Rachel had any idea of the detailed planning and scheduling involved.

We drove from Concepcion to Puerto Montt. Along the way we passed by Temuco which had been the home of Rachel and Georgio when they were married. I asked if she would like to visit the city, perhaps visit with the lawyer who took all their money and house as payment for facilitating Georgio's escaping the death sentence. Rachel reacted with a violent outburst of anger. No, under no conditions would she visit that city! I let the matter drop, and we

RACHEL'S BURNING BUSH

continued to Puerto Montt. Rachel did much of the driving. She wanted to drive, and I really had to make a strong stand in order to take a turn at the wheel. I found it boring being a passenger hour after hour.

When we reached Puerto Montt, we stayed overnight in a hotel in the city and the next day boarded the Patagonia for a high-speed boat ride to the Glaciers. The Patagonia was designed as a hydrofoil and skimmed the top of the water. The ride was rough at times, and the water was very turbulent. I became sea sick and threw up. Rachel held a bag to my mouth as I retched. She tended to me with kindness and caring as she did throughout the trip. We stayed overnight in a lovely, romantic hotel owned by the Patagonia. We went skinny dipping early the next morning and after breakfast took a side trip to a beautiful blue Glacier up on a mountain. I recall walking with Rachel on a swinging, hand-constructed walking bridge beneath which were churning, turbulent waters. On either side of the bridge were green mountains, and except for the sound of water there was an erie silence. The guide took a picture of us standing together in the middle of the bridge. The boat ride to the Glaciers had magnificent scenery. Southern Chile is relatively uninhabited with an occasional Indian family the only sign of human life. The region is marked by silence. Total silence. On either side of the channel were green mountains rising high to the sky. The air was really fresh. It was very pristine.

Finally we arrived at the Glaciers. There were some small icebergs which had broken off from the main glacier and were scattered throughout the region. The main glacier was huge—well over a mile in length, and I don't have any idea of the depth or how far south it extended. The Antarctica is warming (the Greenhouse effect), the Glaciers are melting, and in fifty years they will cease to exist. We disembarked from the main boat into a smaller boat and proceeded to the Glacier, carefully staying a short distance away for fear that a chunk of ice would break apart at any moment. Rachel was thrilled with the venture and full of smiles and laughter.

We flew back to Puerto Montt and drove back to Santiago, stopping overnight at a beautiful, romantic hotel situated in the woods right next to a waterfall. It was perfect for honeymooners. Our room directly overlooked the waterfall which was a few hundred feet away. At night we stood at our picture window and silently became one with nature as the full moon fell on the waterfall. There were no other guests in the adjoining cabins so the only sound we heard was the waterfall. It was soothing to the soul.

When we reached Santiago, we stayed at the Holiday Inn again. I asked for a wake-up call the next morning at 5:30 A.M. to take the hotel shuttle to the airport. At 6:30 A.M., the time the shuttle bus was to leave, we had a knock at our door. It was the driver from the shuttle who was about to leave. The hotel personnel had forgotten to wake us up. We hastily put on our clothes, checked out of the hotel, and boarded the shuttle taxi.

ECUADOR

From Santiago we flew to Quito, Ecuador. I had some difficulty breathing here because of the high altitude—ninety-five hundred feet. Ecuador was very different from the other countries we visited. It has a large indigenous Indian population who seem to be far more gentle than those who traced their ancestry to Europe. The taxi drivers were among the most honest I had encountered on my trip. There seemed to be a kinder, less rushed spirit which permeated the culture.

We stayed in the newest and best hotel in the city, the Oro Verde. Our reservations had been made by the travel agency in Concepcion, Chile and confirmed in writing by a local travel agency in Quito. The price for the room was one hundred dollars. I never thought twice about confirming the price when we checked in since I had a fax with the price on it. The next morning I left Rachel asleep in the room and tried to check out of the hotel early before the rush of other departing guests. This also enabled me to examine the bill more carefully and in a less rushed manner.

The cashier could barely speak English. I

RELATIONSHIP WITH RACHEL

checked the bill and saw the room charge was one hundred fifty dollars per night. Before I did anything else, I told the cashier we had not used anything from the mini bar, and my wife was in bed asleep upstairs and not to disturb her. Unknown to me he disregarded my statement and sent security guards to check out the mini bar in the room to see what we had taken. I refused to pay the one hundred fifty dollar per night charge.

    I went back upstairs to speak with Rachel to see if she could straighten out the problem, since I couldn't carry on a conversation with the cashier in English. When I exited from the elevator, I noticed security guards on the floor. Strange, I thought, I have never seen them on the floor before. I entered the room, and Rachel told me the security guards had entered the room when she was in bed. It was still dark outside. She had jumped out of bed dressed only in a T-shirt and met the men in the middle of the room. The men retreated and left. I became furious. I was protective of Rachel and felt that her privacy had been violated. In addition, I felt that in South America, a woman's honor was involved. Men just do not enter into a woman's room without knocking and waiting an appropriate time. I went back outside and started screaming and yelling at the security guards. They remained quiet.

    I returned to the room. I was more upset about the incident than Rachel. I asked her if she could go

RACHEL'S BURNING BUSH

downstairs and straighten out the room-charge matter. She went downstairs, spoke with the personnel on duty, and listened as the hotel personnel spoke back and forth in Spanish to one another. She learned there were three prices for the same room at the hotel: If you were from Ecuador, the price was fifty dollars; if you were from some other South American country, the price was one hundred dollars; everyone else paid one hundred fifty dollars. We had made our reservation from Chile, and the price given to us was the South American price. When we checked into the hotel, we gave our passports to the hotel personnel at the check-in counter. I have a United States passport, and Rachel had a Spanish passport That was the reason for the one hundred fifty dollar per night charge. Rachel showed them our confirming fax with the charge of one hundred dollars, and they finally reduced the rate to one hundred dollars and took the matter up with the local travel agency. Rachel appeared to be shaken by my anger. Once again another monetary disagreement which followed me everywhere in South America. But there was more to come.

AMAZON

We departed from Quito for our trip to the Amazon. We were picked up by a special bus, traveled for at least an hour to a military airport where

RELATIONSHIP WITH RACHEL

we took a World-War-Two-military-prop plane to the jungle, boarded another bus for a two-hour trip to a boat, and finally boarded this boat for a three-hour trip to another boat. This final boat took us up the Amazon. It was an interesting trip. What I remember most was the side trip to an Indian village and being taken around the jungle by a native guide. I bought a blow gun at the village. Rachel appeared to enjoy the trip to the Amazon.

We returned to Quito but this time stayed at another hotel. Our baggage, however, was dropped off at the first hotel we stayed at. It took the tour operator many hours to locate our baggage.

GALAPAGOS ISLANDS

We went over to the local travel agency responsible for finalizing our trip to the Galapagos Islands. In Concepcion I had paid the travel agency between fifteen hundred and two thousand dollars by credit card for the tour of the Islands. The agency had not been able to write the plane ticket since the airline was owned by Ecuador. I knew the price was around seven hundred fifty dollars for the air fare. (If we had been from Ecuador, the fare would have been around one hundred twenty-five dollars.) I had been assured there would be no problem. The Concepcion-travel agency knew we would only pay by credit card.

The agency in Quito demanded cash payment

for the airline tickets since they said the Ecuador Air Line would not accept credit cards. I turned to Rachel in disbelief. I shook my head—it just couldn't be happening again. "Rachel," I said, "the owner of the agency in Concepcion was a family friend, you knew him, how could he have screwed us?" The fight was knocked out of me. I just didn't have the energy to argue. The high altitude in Quito tired me. I just sat down, defeated, totally frustrated.

Rachel picked up the fight. This time she was upset. While I could have paid the seven hundred fifty dollars, I would have been left dangerously low in funds—probably around one thousand dollars. Rachel asked for our money back on the trip to the Galapagos. The manager came over finally. Without anger, and with a sigh of frustration, I told her of my experiences throughout South America and in Ecuador, and in particular of my pleasant experience with the people of Ecuador. She tried to contact by phone her agency in Chile but was unable to reach them because it was siesta time (noon to about 3:00 P.M. businesses close, but remain open until 7:00 P.M. or 8:00 P.M.). Finally she agreed to do what the Concepcion agency did: she jacked the price up by four percent and put the fare on a credit card.

We were off to the Galapagos Islands. Before we could enter the Islands, we had to pay a forty-five dollar entrance fee per person. The same price would have been fifty cents if we had been from Ecuador.

RELATIONSHIP WITH RACHEL

We flew from Quito to Baltra and then were taken by boat to our cruise boat for our four-day trip to the Islands. Rachel was very helpful on the trip and carried my food tray to our table since my tremor prevented me from doing this myself. The cruise ship would sail to one of the islands, and we would disembark by small motor boat. The animals there were not afraid of man. They had no natural predator and roamed freely. What I remember most vividly were the giant turtles for which the Islands are named, the sea lions which roamed the beach and swam in the water, and the iguanas.

On the first day a motor boat brought us to a beach on one of the Islands where we went swimming. I left early and opted to return on the first boat. Rachel followed shortly thereafter and returned on the boat with me. She was unusually quiet and sat on the opposite end of the boat. After we reboarded the ship, I went to our room to rest. About an hour later, Rachel came into the cabin. I asked her where she had been. She responded: "Do you really want to know? I don't think I should tell you. I don't want you to worry. I have been to the doctor. When I didn't know where you were on the beach, I rushed back to the small ship to see if you were okay. I was thinking of you and if you were okay, and I didn't watch where I was going. I slipped on some rocks and cut myself. I had to have stitches in my mouth and in my gums and I cut my legs."

RACHEL'S BURNING BUSH

Rachel's mouth was beginning to swell and the inside of her mouth was bloody and lacerated. Her legs were also lacerated. I had not noticed this when we were returning to the main ship since she had sat on one end of the small ship, and I had sat on the other end. The physician had given her some pain medication.

But Rachel was also a tough woman who had known hardship. She didn't feel sorry for herself. She showered and went to dinner with me. She continued on as if nothing had happened.

The next morning her mouth and gums were still swollen. We stayed on board the ship that morning. I felt guilty about this mishap. If I had told her where I was going, instead of wandering off, she would not have fallen. It was because of her concern for me that she had fallen. I felt concern about her, protective of her, and was solicitous of her—trying to be helpful if I could.

Just before lunch on the second day, while in our cabin, Rachel erupted from nowhere. I do not recall just what she said; but she was unequivocal about her displeasure with me, her contempt of me and everything about me. Her outburst was intense and took me by surprise. We hadn't been arguing; there hadn't been any disagreement. She was expressing how she felt. I didn't argue with her; I made no attempt to invalidate her feelings or attack her. Instead I told her that if she wasn't happy with me, she didn't have to remain with me. She was free to go. The relationship was not based on servitude, but love and happiness. Since she was obviously not happy with me, I would give her a "divorce." I considered the relationship ended.

She went upstairs for lunch, and I followed her five minutes later. She was sitting having her lunch at one of the tables. Her anger appeared to have subsided, and the look in her eyes indicated she was open to my joining her. I asked a member of the staff to help me with my tray. He started to take me to where Rachel was seated, but I directed him to another table across the room. She looked at me and appeared to be embarrassed by my public display of rejection.

We didn't speak for another whole day except once when I told her she "exhibited a history of self defeat—trying so hard to be good and then chasing away your love objects. You had done that with your two oldest boys, your husband Georgio, and now me. You made life miserable for everyone who got real close to you." She responded by saying that I really knew how to hurt a person. During this time I never saw her in the dining room. We slept in the same cabin but said nothing to one another.

On the second night I was groaning in my sleep. She turned on the light and asked if I was all right. I saw real concern in her face. That was enough to rekindle our relationship. I continued to see Rachel as experiencing a travel-adjustment problem and as manifesting female emotional labileness. Females, in intimate relationships, are prone to emotional swings. You just have to accept it. Her behavior now began to puzzle me, and I sensed the bond between us had changed.

QUITO

When we returned to Quito, we had a few days to travel and see the sights of Ecuador. We hired a guide and went to the Equator. We also went to an Indian market and purchased some personal items for each of us, some items for our families and friends, and some items for our Florida condo. The last day we spent shopping in Quito. I purchased some expensive jewelry for her including a ring. This was a mutual decision.

During the early evening hours, while it was still light, we took a casual walk and stopped at a hotel. I wanted to ask the management of the hotel something and told Rachel I would meet her at the end of the hotel near the hotel cafe. I pointed in the direction to which I was referring. When I finished asking my questions, I walked to where I was to meet her. Rachel was nowhere in sight. I walked back to where I started from in the hotel. Still I couldn't find her. I walked out in the street to the intersection outside the cafe. Still no Rachel. I walked back to our hotel and went up to our room. Still no Rachel. I was starting to panic. I was in a foreign country. I didn't speak the language. Had she been abducted? I went back to the original hotel and had her paged. No response. I called for hotel security and told them what had happened. They decided to walk with me through the hotel.

We found Rachel sitting quietly in a chair against a wall about fifteen feet from where I had left her. She hadn't gone to the end of the hotel at all. She was in a position to see me walk back and forth time and time again. She had not responded to my page. The reason I saw her the last time was that I looked right and left as we walked. She offered no explanation for her behavior.

FLORIDA, MARCH 1992

The next day we flew back to Florida.

We spent a few weeks at my condo, relaxing, fixing up the condo with the items we had purchased, meeting my friends and introducing Rachel to them. It was a pleasant time, and I do not recall any fights or disagreements. Rachel worked hard in cleaning and arranging the apartment, consistent with how a woman would be in fixing up a home for herself and her husband. This was to be her home.

One of my close female friends spent considerable time with Rachel. They talked woman to woman in my friend's condo. Like my other female friends,

RACHEL'S BURNING BUSH

this woman was curious about Rachel and asked Rachel questions to draw her out. My friend told me: "You will never find another woman like Rachel. They broke the mold when they made her. She is the most delightful, sweet, caring, happy, and sensitive person I have ever met. She seemed to be free of the usual psychological problems most people have. I never met a woman so much in love with any man."

A number of events occurred which were significant.

Rachel declared that she thought it best if she left her jewelry at the condo in case she did not come back from Spain. This was obviously a "red flag" that something was wrong. It did not go unnoticed. I had previously made arrangements for us to go to Disney World. I had been there before, and the only reason I had purchased the tickets was to give Rachel the experience.

I told Rachel that the trip to Disney would cost me an extra five hundred dollars. I was doing this only for her. If she wasn't coming back, then please tell me and I would cancel the trip. I didn't want to spend five hundred dollars on someone whom I would never see again. She assured me she was coming back and would like to see Disney World.

A few days later I happened to be speaking on the phone with my brother Esteban. During the discussion he mentioned that his health insurance premium had gone up to five thousand dollars. I knew

RELATIONSHIP WITH RACHEL

I had to purchase health insurance for Rachel. The five thousand dollars really bothered me. I told Esteban he was spending too much, and he should look around for competitive pricing. (He subsequently found equivalent insurance through the Massachusetts Bar Association for around fifteen hundred dollars.) I told Rachel that five thousand dollars was too much to spend.

Rachel's reaction was that she would stay in Spain for four to five months and work to make the five thousand dollars. She didn't want me to spend the money on her. I told her if she did that then we could forget about the relationship. Again it appeared to me that she was looking for a way to break off the relationship. This was the second "red flag." I suggested that instead of her staying in Spain, we would look for a lower-premium-health-insurance policy. I found one for around two thousand dollars.

We went to a local travel agency to see about air fares back to Spain. I thought Rachel might like to go back early without me since all three of her sons would be at home during the last week in April. Jacob, her middle son, was returning from France for one week to celebrate his birthday. I had to remain in the United States to see my cardiologist about my heart condition and my internist on prostate matters. Both physicians were in Boston. These appointments had been arranged months before and were important in view of my past medical history. Rachel wanted to remain in the United States with me rather than return home and be with her sons. She wanted to visit with my cardiologist. "That is my place as your wife," she said.

She only asked to be able to visit with Jacob in France when we returned to Spain. I took this as a statement of unusual love and devotion, and this balanced out in my mind the two previous "red flags" mentioned. I did not dismiss the "red flags" from my mind; but choosing to be with your husband, rather then being with your sons, seemed to me to be a strong indication of strength in the relationship.

The decision on when to return was put on hold. Rachel developed severe headaches and her gums began to bleed (from the fall in the Galapagos). I took her to a local dentist who did some periodontal work on her to stop the bleeding. He advised Rachel that her gums needed the services of a periodontist. The headaches continued and became worse. I took her to a local hospital where they gave her a neurological exam and a CAT scan. Both were negative. Rachel continued to have head pain and her face began to swell. I gave her some antibiotics. This seemed to reduce the swelling, and the pain abated somewhat.

We happened to take a cholesterol exam given free to citizens in the area. My cholesterol was 152, while Rachel's cholesterol was 428 (under 200 is considered good). I panicked. Her headaches had returned, her gums were still bleeding, and now a cholesterol of 428. The 428 really scared me—I thought it was a sign of cardiac problems about to blow up in my face. My own heart condition had made me neurotic about warning signs of heart problems. I gave Rachel some niacin, beginning with 50 mg and working up to 1000 mg in the hope of reducing her cholesterol. I explained to Rachel that niacin could affect the liver, and we had to be on watch for side effects. I decided against going to a local physician because I knew any treatment would have to be carefully monitored, and we had less than a week remaining in Florida.

    I made a decision that Rachel had to go home to Spain for treatment. I was unable to deal with her medical problems and at the same time focus on my own medical tests. (Perhaps if I hadn't been so exhausted from the South American trip, I would have coped better.) She was covered by socialized medicine in Spain, knew the way around the medical establishment in Spain, had her own physicians and dentists who knew her case history, and she could speak to them in Spanish. In the United States it is not easy to make appointments with physicians unless you are a patient. It was difficult for physicians to question Rachel, and I frequently had to act as an interpreter. It was difficult for me to see the pain Rachel suffered and not be able to do anything about it. I had to make a decision quickly. Plane fares were in a state of flux, and I took Rachel to a travel agency and bought her a round-trip ticket from Boston to Barcelona. Rachel felt that I was doing this to "get rid of her," but that wasn't the case. I carefully explained our options. We were both concerned about her head pain. I felt it was best for her to go back to Spain rather than trying to find a physician in the United States. If I had not had my tests to contend with, I would have returned to Spain with her. I assured her I was not abandoning her.

Rachel could not tolerate the niacin, and it was discontinued.

A number of other incidents stand out in my mind. Generally around 5:00 A.M., I used to go for early morning walks. I would quietly dress and try to leave the condo without waking Rachel. If she awoke, she would jump out of bed and ask me to wait for her —so she could go walking with me. I would tell her to go back to sleep, but she wanted to be with me. Another time I went into the kitchen early to make breakfast for us. She awoke; and when she saw what I was doing, she began to cry. This was her job. I left the kitchen and went to take a shower. She always prepared a pleasant breakfast. The last incident involved Rachel, a guest from Boston, and myself. We were talking in the living room. I suggested to Rachel that perhaps she might like to go to the pool or sunbathe by the pool. She looked at me in a strange way and said: "Why should I go out there when you are here!" It was like she always wanted to be with me; keeping me in eye contact.

We drove to Disney World and spent three days there. Rachel thoroughly enjoyed herself—she was like a little girl—smiling happily at the sights.

VIRGINIA

After Disney World we drove to Virginia where her sister lived. I thought it would be nice for the two sisters to spend some time together. We had bought presents for her sister's family in South America. When we arrived at Leah's house, I left Rachel and drove to meet one of my nieces attending school in another part of Virginia. I kept in touch with Rachel by telephone and remember her telling me how much she missed me. When I picked her up three days later, her face was swelling again, and she was in pain. Rachel and her sister agreed that when Rachel returned to the United States from Spain she would spend a week at her sister's house some time in the summer.

We drove back to Boston. We had only one day before Rachel was to leave for Spain. Part of the time I spent opening my mail, paying bills, and putting the apartment in living condition. She finished packing all the sweaters and other things that I had bought for her. She didn't have any money so I gave her nine hundred seventy dollars which represented what was left from the trip. She didn't want to take it. (This was another "red flag," but I didn't catch it.) I told her if she still considered herself to be my wife to take it; if not, leave it. She had to spend a month in Spain before returning to the United States, and she would need spending money. She reluctantly took the money.

On the way to the airport we stopped at Esteban's office. I had sent a package to him from Venezuela, and Esteban had Rachel's Visa credit card. The card had been sent to Rachel by her eldest son in Spain in care of Esteban. By the time it arrived, we were on our way to Mexico. Rachel really looked tired. I looked fine, but Rachel looked like she had been through an ordeal. Her hair was unkempt; her face puffed up; her facial expression not relaxed. Esteban gave me the package. I opened it and couldn't believe what I saw. Although the box was sealed, it had been opened. Whoever had opened the package had removed my clothing and substituted rags. I blew my top again. I turned to Rachel and said something like: "Your people have done it to me again." (While I know it is incorrect, I think of South America as a country, not a continent, and the different countries as states.) Rachel and Esteban drew back at my outburst. Rachel mentioned something to Esteban about my not being able to control my temper. Esteban later mentioned that there was real fury in my face.

RELATIONSHIP WITH RACHEL

We left Esteban's office and drove to the airport. Rachel appeared agitated at the airport. I checked her in, walked to the passenger lounge with her and then said, "Goodbye." As I walked away I turned back a number of times to wave, but she had turned away and appeared to have forgotten about me. I remember thinking that was strange.

CHAPTER 4: ENDING OF RELATIONSHIP

SPAIN, APRIL 1992

As prearranged, Rachel called me when she arrived in Barcelona to let me know she had arrived safely. I spoke to her about a week later. She seemed depressed—her voice sounded strange as if under tension. She said she felt she had abandoned her children by going away with me; that a Jewish-mother's love is very strong, and she was torn between her love of her children and her love for me. I told her to do what was best for her. Her happiness was my concern. Whatever would make her happy was what she should do. If she wasn't happy with me, she should remain in Spain. She responded by saying that she was always happy with me even when we argued. She said she loved me, would always love me, she was my wife, would always be my wife, would always be married to me. She also mentioned that her washing machine was broken, and she had to buy a new machine which would cost about seven hundred dollars. This was another reason for her staying in Spain—to work to accumulate enough money to buy the machine. She did not want money from me. Despite her comment I sent her a check for one thousand dollars so she could buy the machine. I also wrote her a letter indicating I loved her and wanted her.

A week later I spoke to her again. She felt that she was going to remain in Spain. I recall her saying something like this: As of 7:30 P.M. on (whatever the

ENDING OF RELATIONSHIP

date was) she had decided to remain in Spain. She said it like a joke—like it was funny to her. I thought to myself: how weird, how callous. I told her that I had purchased a plane ticket to Barcelona to make sure she was okay. I wondered if this decision on her part was not covering up something she wanted to shield from me. She pleaded with me not to come. She couldn't resist me. Seeing me would be too stressful for her. She had to remain in Spain for her children. I sent her a second letter stating that I was coming over not to take her back, but to make sure I was not abandoning her in her time of need. If she was all right, I would leave. I would not force her to return. But I wanted to make sure that I had acted in a responsible manner to her and not abandoned her if something was wrong.

I had such trust in Rachel that it was inconceivable that she might be lying to me.

The next time we spoke she told me that her son, Jacob, had been hospitalized but was improved and at home now. She also advised me that she would not pick me up at the airport in Barcelona; I could not stay at her house; she would speak to me; the marriage was over with; she was divorcing me; and I could rent a car and travel around Spain while I was in the country. Her tone was cold and impersonal and without feelings. I can still recall my body and head jerking convulsively at each of her statements: "I will not pick you up!" .... "You can't stay at my house!"

RACHEL'S BURNING BUSH

.... "I am divorcing you!" .... "The marriage is over with!" I was stunned. I asked her why she was hurting me. She replied she wasn't hurting me but was hurting us. She mentioned she had a job as a tour guide (which would take her away from her home for weeks at a time).

This flip-flop in behavior all happened within a little over two weeks of her returning to Spain. It didn't make any sense to me. Here was a woman, age fifty, who appeared to be "dumping" a man who loved her. Her lover was kind, considerate, sensitive, tender, affluent, considered handsome, a gentleman of high integrity. She could live in the United States in a state of luxury, not have to work, travel part of the year, visit Spain and be with her sons part of the year (for a longer period of time than her previous job allowed her). She would have few more chances. She was abandoning both her children and the man she loved. She had gone from a state of foregoing being with her sons and celebrating her son Jacob's birthday so that she could be with the man she loved, to ending the relationship with the man she supposedly loved, to taking a job that entailed abandoning her sons, all within a matter of weeks without any intervening event to explain such a change.

When I first met her on board the Omega, she indicated to me she took the job to enable her children to become independent from her. She was now claiming she had to remain in Spain to be with her children. This was obviously not true since she claimed she had taken a job as a tour guide which would take her away from her children for weeks at a time. She was not telling me the truth; but even this didn't make any sense. It was a stupid lie. She just could have said to me she wasn't happy, the language and cultural difference were too much; she realized this when she returned home; she had a wonderful time with me, and she was sorry for hurting me. Finis. It was her inconsistencies and lies which prompted me to investigate further.

I decided it was fruitless to go to Spain to see her. The bottom line was that she wanted to end the relationship. I had my brother, Esteban, call her and tell her I was not coming and ask her to return the money I had given and sent her. Esteban's reaction to the thirty-minute phone call he had with Rachel was that she was not depressed; I was past history, and she was moving on to something else. This was all within three weeks of returning to Spain. She told Esteban she was going to send me a letter explaining what had happened in detail and send a copy to him.

She sent me a three-page letter and enclosed the money I had given her. (She also sent a copy of the letter to Esteban.) Our reaction to the letter was that it was hollow and insincere. Rachel began by saying she had hurt her sons as well as me by her behavior. I was the finest gentleman she had ever known, kind, sensitive, and caring. In her country a woman takes a mother's degree when she has children. She stays with them until they leave the house. When she returned home her children told her how much they missed her, and they felt she had abandoned them. It was one thing to leave home to work for your family, but to leave home with a man for your own pleasure was abandoning your children. She was torn apart by her childrens' comments. A mother's love is very strong. She had to remain home for her children. She was thankful that I didn't come over to Spain because she couldn't resist me. The letter didn't ring true. There were all the right words, but there was no feeling or emotion behind them.

 I called her sister Leah in Virginia to find out if during their discussion Rachel had mentioned a problem in our relationship. Her sister appeared to be as stunned as I was. Rachel had agreed to visit with her sister in a few months when she returned to the United States. Leah thought possibly that hormonal changes associated with a woman's change in life might be responsible for Rachel's behavior.

 I called her son Jacob in France. It was my feeling that sudden changes in behavior were frequently associated with organic disease. The Rachel I knew was not the same Rachel I had spoken with on the phone in Spain. I did not believe the story about mother's love, nor did I believe her coldness was a defense mechanism. I didn't exist for her anymore. Jacob stated there was no physical problem. His

ENDING OF RELATIONSHIP

mother had originally told him that she was going away with me to enable her sons to become independent. She was now telling her sons she ended the relationship with me in order to stay with her sons. The reason I couldn't stay in their house was because she couldn't resist me. If I stayed in the house, her resolve would melt away and she would return to the United States with me. She had to stay in Spain for her children. Jacob stated that was the way his mother was. There was no logic to his mother's behavior; she could swing from one emotional state to another abruptly without reason. She was all emotion. It was because she was so emotional that people liked her. His parting comment to me was to forget about his mother—that you cannot have a relationship with someone whose emotions you cannot trust.

MY EMOTIONAL REACTION TO RACHEL'S DECISION

I was confused, angry and in anguish. I had trusted Rachel completely. In fact it was the trust which was the foundation of the relationship. This chaotic and tumultuous ending was beyond my imagination. To me, to my friends and family who had met her—she gave every indication of being a woman deeply in love.

I found the reaction of my brother and friends interesting. They were operating from information

RACHEL'S BURNING BUSH

they had at hand. They knew Rachel as a sweet, nice, unselfish, unsophisticated woman who was obsessionally in love with me. They sought an explanation not in Rachel, but in something I must have done to her to cause her to end the relationship. My brother Esteban and close female friends with whom I spoke all supported Rachel. They felt I was wrong in sending her back to Spain alone for medical tests. They felt I had abandoned her. The women felt that if this had happened to them, they would have ended the relationship. I shook my head in disbelief. They knew about my heart condition. Did they really feel that I should have canceled my medical appointments with my cardiologist and internist and returned to Spain with Rachel? They answered: "I was thinking logically, and with a woman you have to consider emotions." What I didn't know at the time was that my brother and female friends had abandonment issues of their own.

LETTER TO RACHEL

I wrote Rachel the following very strong letter.

Dear Rachel,

Everyone that I have spoken with about what has happened between us has indicated that your story is not the whole truth.

ENDING OF RELATIONSHIP

You indicated to me while we were in Spain that the reason you went on board the ship, rather than working in Barcelona, was to separate yourself from your boys to enable them to free themselves from you and become independent. This was a sacrifice you made as a mother. It was for the good of your children. I accepted this.

In Spain you also indicated to me that the reason for your husband's suicide had to do with his discovering latent homosexual feelings. I felt the subject was too sensitive and inappropriate to probe further because it was obviously one of great pain for you.

While we travelled in South America, you indicated to me that I was your "Burning Bush," you would never abandon me, we would spend not only this life together but all eternity, you loved me too much, you were happy with me, you just wanted to be wherever I was, you were my wife, my family was your family and your family was my family, and you would never hurt me.

I trust my brother Esteban one hundred percent; but I trusted you more. I trusted you like I trusted my own mother.

Everyone understands the pull of a mother's love. Everyone understands that when a son is sick, a mother's instinct is to be with her child and take care of him. Everyone understands the difficulty in being separated from your children over vast distances.

RACHEL'S BURNING BUSH

Everyone understands the cultural and language difficulty that you faced.

What no one understands is your behavior. A woman really in love would have attempted to see if I would be willing to spend more time in Spain. (I only spend a few months of the year in Boston to have my annual check-ups.) You made a unilateral decision that this was not an option. After the first week in Spain, you indicated you were probably going to remain in Spain; but you would always love me and always be married to me. By the end of the second week in Spain, you indicated you would not pick me up at the airport, I should rent a car, you would speak to me face to face, but I should not stay in your house but rather travel around Spain, the marriage was over with and you were divorcing me. Your voice was cold and controlled and completely lacking in empathy for the pain you were inflicting on me. Indeed, I had become the enemy.

I recognize that I really did not know you at all. Your actions make no sense to me or anyone else that I have spoken with. At least one person has indicated you were a gold digger. This was a very expensive trip Rachel. As of now the cumulative bills amount to over thirty-three thousand dollars. Direct expenditures on you—travel, trips, meals, jewelry, clothes, presents amounted to over fifteen thousand dollars. I exclude hotel bills because I would have incurred that expense without you.

ENDING OF RELATIONSHIP

When Esteban spoke with you, he sensed you were sad but not depressed. You expressed concern about what the doctor had to say about my heart but no concern or compassion about my feelings. He sensed your attitude toward me was more clinical as opposed to emotional concern. I was already part of your past and forgotten.

Ruth has indicated to me that you told her your husband's suicide was related to his socialist friends in Chile making death threats against him.

You have indicated to me that the reason you took the job on the boat was to provide for your family. As I remember it, the money you earned on the ship went to reduce the mortgage.

Rachel, there are too many inconsistencies here. It is difficult for me to believe you are a con artist, you were insincere, you are a pathological liar. I know you were depressed following your husband's suicide, but have you been hospitalized for psychiatric reasons? I think there is a lot more to your husband's suicide than you have told me.

My own psychological state is very poor. I have regressed and experiencing psychomotor agitation, repeated and sustained periods of anguish, loneliness and suicidal feelings. You have no idea of the depth of psychological problems you have precipitated; and what is even more interesting, you couldn't care less.

The whole purpose of this letter is to ask you to tell me the truth. At least with the truth and the whole story I can begin to put my life back together. When we were together, your attitude toward me was extreme. You stuck to me like a puppy dog. You couldn't do enough for me. Your love knew no limits. You didn't care where we went as long as we were together. Within just a matter of days of returning to Spain, this attitude flip flopped; and you decided never to see me again. The behavior here is too extreme and is not explained by a mother's love. No one buys this. I have no doubt that one of your sons, probably Isaac, made you feel some guilt about leaving. But you are an adult and should be capable of withstanding the selfish manipulation of a twenty-three-year-old son. He is no longer a young boy saying that he didn't ask to be brought into this world. The role of every parent is to let go and let the adult children establish their own lives.

There is something else at work here. I think it is psychiatric in nature. The mood swings are too great. Can you tell me now the whole story? What really caused your husband's suicide? What were your real feelings toward me? What are you really feeling now? Are you relieved that it is all over? Were you ultimately the biggest thief that I ran into in South America—someone who sensed a lonely person on the ship, who wanted a nice time and saw me as a vehicle for her pleasure, who used me and then discarded me? Your story is not a story of love, but rather pathology. I would like to know the real Rachel.

ENDING OF RELATIONSHIP

I have returned to you a package of some of your personal clothing you left here. I think it would be proper for you to return to me, in addition to the nine hundred seventy dollars, the jewelry, the sweaters and table cloth you were sewing. In fact if you were a real mensch, you would return everything including the presents I bought for your children.

I do not think you remotely understand how inappropriate your behavior was. According to the original Jewish law, marriage is a private matter between two people. It has nothing to do with civil law. The clergy did not enter the picture until the middle ages. It is a commitment two people make to one another for life. You went on a honeymoon with me for almost four months. Even toward the end when the subject of Disney World came up, I asked you if you were coming back. I told you this was going to cost me five hundred dollars, I had seen Disney World before, and I didn't want to pay this if you were not coming back to me. When I gave you the nine hundred seventy dollars, I asked you the same question. In both cases you assured me you were coming back. You even deceived your sister; you told her you would visit her for a week in June. You even told Ann that it was your intent to live in Boston with me, and you felt sadness about leaving me and returning to Spain. You told her you felt I was abandoning you.

If a person was being honest and of sound mind,

it is impossible to behave to someone you love in the manner you did. You do not go on a four-month honeymoon involving Florida, Mexico and South America where your husband spent lavishly on you and then within two weeks of returning to Spain tell him the marriage is over, you will not even pick him up at the airport, and he cannot stay at your house. If I did something to you to warrant such behavior by you, I would like to hear what I did. I am so deaf, dumb, and blind that I thought I showed you love, caring, and tenderness. What you did to me was outright cruel. It wasn't so much what you did, but how you did it, and how you handled it. One of the things that is characteristic of you is that you lack tact. Another thing that is also characteristic of you is that you lack empathy. You feel no guilt about what you have done to me or how you have treated me. You rationalize what you have done by saying that you also feel pain, and you have not done anything to me but to us.

You took a man who had been under psychiatric care for agitated depression resulting from a breakup with one woman and the death of his mother, plus the death of his brother—all of these events occurring within the past year—and discarded him as if he didn't exist. When I met you on board the ship, I was very vulnerable. I was just coming out of my depression, and the anguish was beginning to lessen. While I was lonely, I was beginning to stand on my two feet. When you left Boston, you knew you were not returning.

ENDING OF RELATIONSHIP

You should have had the decency of telling me the truth and leaving the things in Boston. Instead you took everything but the hat I bought you in Mexico. You were careful to take the pictures of your sons—a tip off that you knew you were not coming back. In the end I was treated like a bill collector—you would see me face to face, but then I should leave your house and travel around Spain. I feel you treated me like shit. The cost to purchase the plane ticket to Spain plus transportation to and from the Boston airport came to over seven hundred dollars. This was a lot of money to spend, not to convince you to come home, but to make sure that you and your children were okay, and that I was not abandoning you in time of need. When you subsequently dissolved our marriage, told me to rent a car and/or fly around Spain, and indicated I should not stay in your house—this escalated my costs to over two thousand dollars. To spend this amount of money under the circumstances would have been masochistic.

    Many people are moved initially by the emotion of mother's love. How sacrificial and tragic to have to choose between your children and the man you love! If you buy into this argument, then you really put down women. Women, under this thesis, are not responsible for their behavior. It is their prerogative in matters of love and feeling to change their mind under any and all circumstances. Erratic behavior is condoned because a person is a woman. Commitment to another person is excused because you are a woman. This is nonsense and a put down of women! The time to choose between your children and the man you love is before you make a commitment not after you spend a four-month honeymoon with a man. You chose to separate yourself from your children prior to meeting me—by taking a job on a cruise ship. Fickle behavior is not the right of women.

As you can see, I am angry at being taken. If there had been a real bond between us, you would have tried to work out a solution with me. When Jacob became ill, if there had been a bond between us, you would have called me to share your problem. But that is not your style. Your style is to retreat into yourself and live in your own world. When you are under stress, no one can touch you, and you resort to outward calm and control.

It is the feeling here in Boston among professionals that I have consulted that I should not count on receiving the money and jewelry as promised. They feel this erratic behavior you have exhibited would only repeat itself if you changed your mind, and I would be better off without you. They have indicated if you did return you would repeatedly cause me stress, grief, and misery because of your instability. It was interesting to me that they used the word misery because that was the same word I used to describe your behavior. No one believes your story about the children. They think that is part of it, but the real

ENDING OF RELATIONSHIP

truth lies somewhere else. If possible I would like to know.

I am beginning to understand why Georgio took his own life. You do not seem to understand how you interact with your loved ones. You make supreme sacrifices for them and then you make their lives miserable with some craziness that you focus on. In the end they take their own lives like Georgio did, are unable to break away from you like Isaac has done, or strike out on their own like Jacob did. You are really very clever at what you do, although I do not think you do this at a conscious level. Everyone that meets you likes you. You are sweet and nice and kind and good. But no one really knows the real Rachel until they live with you. Remember, I used to call you the president of the Vilda Meshuggener Society?

Somewhere there is an unconscious need to punish yourself. It probably is traceable to the relationship you had with your parents. Your emotions fluctuate from being rigidly controlled to being labile and extreme.

I end this letter with a story. It took place in Nazi Germany. There was a woman who was starving and too weak to even eat. The Nazis befriended this woman. They showed her kindness and gentleness and coaxed her to eat. She at first refused but relented in face of the benevolence showed. After she had eaten the meat they gave her, they told her that they had killed her daughter, and the meat she had just eaten was the flesh of her own daughter. Can you imagine the emotions of this mother.

That's the pain I feel.

I was very lonely and needy when you met me. You showed me love without limits: you left your job, your children, your house and your friends to be with me. No woman, even my own mother, could have been as kind, loving, caring, and solicitous as you were on our trip. You lulled me into a state of complete trust in you. I could never imagine you leaving me. And then you pulled the rug from underneath me.

Have a good life Rachel.

REACTION OF MY BROTHER AND FRIENDS TO MY LETTER

I showed the letter to my brother and some friends. Their comments and reactions were all very similar. They thought it was the most devastating and destructive letter they had ever read! They were dumb struck by it. The end of the letter, where I spoke of the mother unknowingly eating the flesh of her child, was particularly heinous and upsetting to them. Everyone, after reading the letter, sort of took a deep breath, raised their eyes and looked at me without speaking. They were initially speechless and dealing with their own emotional response to the letter.

My brother commented he hoped I hadn't sent the letter. He felt it was a cruel letter. In particular

ENDING OF RELATIONSHIP

he chastised me for the Nazi reference. He felt it was very inappropriate to link Rachel's behavior with the Nazis. Her entire family had been killed by the Nazis. To suggest a connection between Rachel and the Nazis was abhorrent and obtuse. Didn't I understand the emotional pain this would cause her? In addition I had, in effect, stated that she was responsible for her husband's death. Hadn't this woman suffered enough?

Other friends made similar comments. They all indicated that this letter would certainly end the relationship, and my letter would be answered. It was too strong to go unanswered.

I listened to the comments without much emotion. I felt that they had all missed the point. I was suffering indescribable pain. I had bonded with Rachel; she was now my life. She had become my "burning bush." I had trusted her completely. This betrayal of trust struck at my very soul. The Nazi story was my way of describing my pain. It was not designed to hurt Rachel. Every single friend and family member, with the exception of a female cousin and niece, could not understand my pain and suffering. They saw it as a relationship ending, and I should go on with my life. They really showed more sympathy toward Rachel than toward me.

It was and is my position that one of the definitions of a friend is being able to validate your feelings. Validation does not mean agreeing with. It means simply understanding and not disapproving of the emotions you are feeling. It does not mean giving you advice when you are in great pain—unless you ask for it. According to this restrictive definition, most of us are lucky if we have one or two friends. It was clear I didn't have any adult friends. The relationship with Rachel showed me just how alone I was in the world.

My so called friends were right about one thing. I did receive an answer.

RACHEL'S REPLY

Apparently by the time my letter arrived in Spain (probably less than a month from the time she left the United States), Rachel was gone. She was traveling around Spain as a tour guide. About a month later (two months from the time she left the United States), I received a letter from Seville—almost one thousand miles from Barcelona where she lived. Her son had opened my letter and described the contents. Her letter was full of anger. She stated she couldn't stand my way of life. It was an emotional, rambling letter full of sound and fury but of no substance or logic. It wasn't that her English was poor or her spelling inaccurate—that would be expected—her letter reflected, by its contents and ideas, an uneducated person—someone who probably had not graduated from high school and did unskilled work for a living. That is the way the letter struck me anyway.

ENDING OF RELATIONSHIP

About a month later I received a second letter. This time she was in Italy. Her son had sent my letter to her, and she was directly responding now. The second letter was more of the same. Rachel now claimed she didn't love me anymore. I had destroyed any love she had for me by my letter. She listed a number of reasons for ending the relationship. These included my angry outbursts and frustrations: Did I remember trying to kick the door down at the American Airlines' office in Buenos Aires when they closed the door at 5:00 P.M. just as I approached. She couldn't stand my teasing her in general and specifically about her English; and my talk of past girl friends. She felt I had abandoned her when she was ill, used her as a cook, translator, and driver; and never really loved her. She claimed I tried to kill her with niacin when her cholesterol was elevated. She wanted to know why I wanted to take a nude photograph of her. She stated she was afraid of me. I was a dangerous man. I was mentally ill. I would never know how much I had hurt her. She also stated she would be home in November (this was now July).

REACTION OF FRIENDS AND FAMILY TO RACHEL'S LETTER

Again, my friends and family supported Rachel. They understood clearly why she had ended the relationship. I was a bad man. I didn't understand women. Women are frightened by a man's anger whether or not it is directed at them; they don't like to be teased; they don't like to be used in a servile manner; they are jealous of past relationships with other women; they need to know a man will not abandon them when they are ill; they need to feel secure in a home and not just travel. I had a lot to learn about women.

I listened in disbelief. These people knew me. Was I really a bad man, a dangerous man? They had all experienced displays of my anger and my teasing. Were they afraid of me? Did they find my teasing demeaning? Did they not recognize my sensitivity, empathy, and emotional support? Did they not see the man whom they had turned to for help and insight when faced with adversity? Sure I had some character flaws; I was no icon. But on balance was their view of me positive or negative?

Their answers surprised me. In general they indicated I was a strong man, very secure, erudite and more mentally healthy than most people they knew. Their sympathy toward Rachel was based on their view of Rachel as a person who had suffered a great deal and who was trying to put her life back together. Their lack of sympathy toward me was that they saw me in opposite terms—strong, decisive, logical, in charge. I gave the impression of being autonomous and needing no one, while Rachel gave an opposite impression.

CHAPTER 5: INVESTIGATION OF RACHEL

SUMMER AND FALL, 1992

Over the summer and into the fall I continued to be in emotional pain and confused by the ending. I didn't believe any of her letters. I went about my life. I dated for a very short time a woman who was the opposite of Rachel. She had a Ph.D., was a successful entrepreneur, a self-made millionaire, who had graduated number one in her class at Harvard.

I was amused that this woman, who was obviously my intellectual superior, who was on the M.I.T faculty, who dealt on a regular basis with the best and brightest minds, felt that I was one of the deepest thinkers she knew. She felt I liked to play the role of a simple, naive, vulnerable person, but this was a deceptive mask—that I never spoke without considering a point from six different positions. I knew exactly where I was going, knew exactly what I wanted, and was in control at all times. I calmly moved people around like pawns. I was very good and very clever at what I did. I always took time to listen to another person. I focused my attention on the speaker as if he or she was important. I always validated a person's emotions. I didn't disagree or offer advice. I just listened and asked questions that indicated validation of the speaker. I made the person feel important and understood. And then I moved them intellectually in any direction I wanted. I am not sure how much of this is valid or projection on the part of this brilliant woman. In any case it amused me that someone of her talent took me seriously. I certainly don't feel all that powerful, confident, and manipulative.

I couldn't put the Rachel matter to rest. There was something missing here. It didn't make sense to me. Despite what Rachel said in her letters, despite her pejorative comments on my personality, I knew in the main that I had treated her with love, kindness, and caring. I felt she had treated me in the same way. Despite our occasional arguments, we had a good time together. Pictures that I had taken throughout our travel showed Rachel with a happy, ear-to-ear smile. I had really tried hard to give as much as I received, not just in the money I spent on Rachel, but also by listening, caring, kindness and love.

It was my feeling that to forget, you must first forgive, and in order to forgive you must first understand. Rachel's second letter mentioned she would be back in Spain in November. I called Spain and spoke with her son. He said she was in Greece and wouldn't be back until November. Now the plot seemed to involve subterfuge. If she was in Greece and she wouldn't be home until November, then she was back on one of the cruise ships. Her story about staying home for her children was an outright lie. I couldn't understand what was going on.

Here was a woman who for five months demonstrated obsessional love for me. When it came

INVESTIGATION OF RACHEL

time for her to go home and be with her children and seek medical attention, she wanted instead to remain with me in Boston while I underwent my medical tests. When she returned to Spain, she stated she felt obligated to remain in Spain and stay with her children. She promptly forgot about me, then turned around and abandoned her children and returned to the cruise ship. Was there another man involved? If so, what was the explanation for her obsessional love while we were together? When she returned to Spain, did some past lover contact her from the ship, and she went away with him?

Whatever the reason, I needed closure. I needed to see Rachel, face to face, and find out the truth. I decided to combine a trip to Portugal and Morocco with a stop over in Spain. The trip was planned for early November 1992.

SPAIN, NOVEMBER 1992

All my family and friends advised me not to see Rachel in Spain. Their advice was to let go, the relationship was over. They saw my behavior as obsessional and not in my best interest. I could only get hurt. They brought up the question of my self-esteem: why was I allowing this woman to have so much control over my life? One female friend, who had been abandoned by her husband for another woman, identified with Rachel (she felt that I had

RACHEL'S BURNING BUSH

abandoned Rachel) and mentioned she was thinking of writing to Rachel to warn her I was coming: "We women have to stick together," she said. This woman further warned me that Rachel might call the police on me—that's what she would do under the circumstances.

The disapproval of family and friends compounded my emotional pain. I internalized their disapproval. Their opinions had validity. I recognized the obsessive nature of my behavior, and the risk of implementing my plan. I would be entering an alien environment; I did not speak Spanish; I had no idea what I would find; I didn't even know if Rachel would be at home; I didn't know if she would even speak with me; and though I had been there, I wasn't even sure how to find her house.

Nevertheless I remained undaunted. It has always been my position that knowledge is power and freedom, and that mystery and benightedness is bondage. Truth sets a person free. I have counseled others facing similar situations according to this doctrine. I could not remain true to myself if I did not practice what I preached.

Frankly I went to Spain with trepidation. My heart was at peace, however. I felt no enmity toward Rachel. She chose what was best for her. That was her right. I feared the worst: she wouldn't see me; she was living with another man; she would call the police. But I had to take the risk and put the Rachel

INVESTIGATION OF RACHEL

issue behind me.

Rachel had given my brother Esteban a set of keys to her house. Neither Esteban nor I are sure why this was done. In any case he gave me the keys. I flew from Boston via TWA to Barcelona and then rented a car. I first stopped at my hotel to shower, shave, and change my clothes. It was early afternoon when I arrived at her house. I rang the bell, but there was no answer. Finally I used her keys to gain entry into the house. The house was cold. I don't mean temperature. I am referring to a coldness associated with a lack of human activity. I went into the kitchen and opened the refrigerator door. A few old cold cuts were in evidence. I went to Rachel's bedroom. It looked like it hadn't been used. There was no sign of activity. I looked for the box of clothes and other things I had given her. It was not there. There were no pictures in the bedroom. (When I had visited her a year ago, she had a few pictures in her room.) I went to her bathroom. Again, no sign of activity. The living room gave no sign of use. I went upstairs to her sons' bedrooms. Again no sign of activity other than unmade beds. I left the house and returned a few hours later.

It was late afternoon when I returned to the house. Her oldest and youngest sons were at home. The front door was open, and I entered as her oldest son came to the door. He looked surprised (understandably) and nervous. We sat down and engaged in light talk. They indicated Rachel was in Barcelona and not at home. I didn't quite understand this. I took this to mean she was not living at home. I therefore invited her sons out to dinner the next evening (remember I had no ill-will to Rachel or her boys). They accepted. I thought they would enjoy a good meal rather than the cold cuts they were living on. Finally, it came out that Rachel would be back that evening.

We continued to speak. They were tense, ill at ease, and cautious. I told them I was visiting Portugal and Morocco and thought I would stop in and say, "Hello." I was still operating from the mind set and emotions of when Rachel and I were together. They mentioned that Rachel had been working again for the Olympus Cruise ship on board the Iliad—the smallest of the ships. She was scheduled to sail on the Piraeus that winter. I said that didn't make any sense. She indicated she had to stay in Spain for her children. They responded she couldn't find a job in Spain. I countered with the statement this had been the season of the summer Olympics in Barcelona. Certainly with her multi-language ability she could have found a job as a tour guide in Barcelona. They parried back that this would have been only for the summer. I dropped the matter. It was inappropriate for me to discuss the matter with her children.

Her sons thought Rachel would be home shortly. I waited until 7:30 P.M. It was dark by then, and I was tired. They mentioned they left for school in the morning (6:30 A.M.), and Rachel would be at home in the morning. I told them I would be back around 8:00 A.M. I returned to my hotel about a mile away. I dreamt of being together with Rachel again. This was not my intent when I decided to visit her, but being so close to her reawakened old emotions.

When I arrived at her house the next morning, the house was in darkness. It was about 7:00 A.M. I figured her sons had left, and Rachel was still in bed. Rather than waking her by ringing the bell, I decided to use her keys. She had double locked the door, and the keys did not work. I had to resort to ringing the bell. She met me in great anger and demanded the return of her keys which I promptly gave to her. Her sons had overslept and were still upstairs. She quickly showered and changed into a business suit. My initial reaction to her was that she appeared hard and tough. She had let her hair grow so that there was more hair than face. There was nothing soft or feminine about her. We talked for a short while. She began the conversation asking about my heart. It was asked without real concern—like someone saying to you, "Hi, how are you?" and not really caring. At around 7:30 A.M. she received a phone call from a man she identified as Roberto. She spoke in English to the man. As was usual in her conversations, the other party did most of the talking. I was unable to pick up the gist of the conversation. I did notice that Isaac, her oldest son, had a disturbed look on his face while his mother spoke. The conversation appeared to upset him. He knew who it was. It is unusual in Spain for someone to speak English on the phone. Rachel stated that it was her American boss from the tour company for whom she worked. (I later learned she hadn't worked for the tour company for many months; many months later she claimed she never worked for the tour company. In any case, I concluded the call was probably from a man with whom she was having a relationship.)

Rachel said she could not speak with me very long. She had an appointment and told me to come back later in the morning. I offered to drive her, but she emphatically declined—with a great deal of anger. There was something very wrong, but I had no idea what it was. I returned about 9:30 A. M., and we spoke.

The conversation did not go well. I remained calm and soft spoken—mindful of the admonition I had received about the possibility of her calling the police. She, on the other hand, was tense and angry. She denied her son's story about being on the Iliad. She had not been in Greece. She had not worked on board any cruise ship. She didn't have any idea why her son told me this story—probably to protect her. She worked as a tour-guide and had been to France. She returned every few weeks to her home outside Barcelona. While she had a job offer to go on the

INVESTIGATION OF RACHEL

Piraeus that winter, she was scheduled to go to Eastern Europe as a tour guide in a few weeks. I left after about an hour with my head ringing. She resisted answering many of my questions, stating she felt I was interrogating her. Many times I would ask a question, only to be met with silence. She would just look at me as if I said nothing. She exhibited no sign of discomfort, no sign of anxiety, just a look as if she was waiting for me to say something.

I went back to my hotel, had some lunch, and went upstairs to rest. But I was too agitated to rest and decided to return and see if I could derive some closure. Rachel was resting in bed when I returned. She invited me into her house, and we talked in a more friendly manner.

With tears running down her face, she said she still loved me, would always love me; there would never be any other man in her life; she was still my wife, would always be my wife; she would always be married to me, but I had abandoned her. Her marital status was that of being married but without a husband. Her husband had left her. I accepted these comments as coming from the president of the Avilda Meshuggener Society.

During our conversation Rachel stated that her physician had discovered a thyroid insufficiency, and she was now on thyroid pills. She had lost twenty pounds since going on the pills. In addition, her cholesterol was now 150. Her physician had detected

RACHEL'S BURNING BUSH

a lump in her neck, and she was to have a biopsy to determine if it was malignant. She also mentioned she was seeing an endocrinologist—her physicians felt that she might have something wrong with her glands that was causing the thyroid to malfunction.

I made an attempt to feel her throat to feel the lump to which she was referring. She pulled away and wouldn't let me touch her. She wouldn't even allow me to touch her hand. No physical contact was allowed.

I told her if the results of her biopsy indicated she had cancer and she needed someone to take care of her, I would return to Spain and see what I could do. If her physicians felt the best treatment was in the United States, I would pay for the treatment. This really was a significant gesture on my part and could have cost me a few hundred thousand dollars. At times I can be penurious, but when it is for something important—such as a person's life—then money is unimportant.

At some point in the conversation, Rachel suddenly began to show nystagmus ocular movements. I sensed a metamorphosis occurring right before my eyes. The old Rachel was returning. Instead of the coldness she had exhibited toward me, she asked me if I would like some tea. We went into the kitchen and hugged while she was making the tea.

We returned to the livingroom to have our tea. As the conversation continued, she withdrew into her

INVESTIGATION OF RACHEL

shell again.

Rachel said she had just sent the jewelry and clothing to Esteban. "Why did you send it to my brother?" I asked. She didn't answer. She just looked at me. No shrug. Nothing. It was as if I didn't ask the question.

Since she returned the jewelry I had bought her, I thought it proper to return the jewelry she had bought me for Valentine's Day. She refused to accept it back. She said she gave it to me in love, and she wanted me to keep it as a token of her love. I left it on the table and returned to my car. She followed me out to my car. When I opened the car door, she put the jewelry into the car and went back into her house. I stopped, took out the jewelry, placed it outside her house, and drove off.

It was a strange afternoon—to say the least. Certainly not everything made sense. I wanted closure, so I believed what she told me. I concluded she was caught in a dilemma between the love of her sons and her love of me. Mother's love was strongest.

When I was in Portugal, I called her about her biopsy. She claimed it was negative.

RETURN TO BOSTON, DECEMBER 1992

When I returned to the United States and told some of my friends what had happened, they felt that Rachel had been untruthful. A woman in love would not have acted that way. They thought the story was crazy. Now my friends and family, who up to now were sympathetic toward Rachel, became suspicious of her real motive and saw her as a sick person. They seemed to react with far more intense negative vibes about Rachel than I did. The drama of her telling me she loved me, with tears running down her face, was very moving and convincing. I was reacting emotionally to the person, while they were reacting to the story.

A few days after returning to the United States, I called her at 7:30 A.M. Spanish time. I called to find out the results from the endocrinologist. There was no answer. I thought to myself—that is strange, I wonder if her son was telling me the truth. I called the Olympus Cruise office in Greece. They told me she was on the Piraeus due to arrive in Fort Lauderdale, Florida on December 20th. They also told me she had been on the Iliad that summer. The Piraeus was not due back to Greece until late April or early May.

I was stunned. I had been lied to by someone whom I had completely trusted. As I was to subsequently learn, almost everything she told me was a lie. She had nothing wrong with her thyroid and never had a biopsy.

Nothing made any sense to me or to any of my family or friends with whom I consulted.

The Rachel I traveled with was a happy, kind, nurturing woman; she interacted well with others; she

INVESTIGATION OF RACHEL

appeared to be very much in love with me; she did not exhibit serious psychopathology when we were together; her neighbors in Spain appeared to like her; the staff and passengers on the ship we were on in Greece thought well of her; her friends in Concepcion, Chile where she grew up greeted her with warmth and were excited to see her; her in-laws in Santiago, Chile treated her with the love you would associate with a favorite daughter; my own friends and family were enchanted with her and viewed her as too unsophisticated to be capable of mendacity, duplicity, or deception. She had spent over four months with me traveling around South America visiting many of the places she would have seen if she had been a social hostess on the Piraeus. By going with me, she had given up five thousand dollars in wages which she could have used to reduce her mortgage. Just weeks before returning to Spain, she opted to stay in the United States and visit with my cardiologist in Boston rather than return to her home and be with her three sons when her middle son Jacob returned from France in celebration of his birthday. She had returned nineteen hundred seventy dollars which I had given her as well as all the clothes and jewelry which I had bought for her.

When she returned home and told me about how much she had missed her children and was thinking about staying in Spain, I told her to do what was best for her—what would make her happy and cause her the least pain. I told her I loved her, wanted her, would be willing to reach a compromise—but her decision should be based on what was in her best interest.

There was no reason that I could see to lie to me. I had given her an escape window to use. She could have said simply that she realized when she arrived home how much she missed her language, culture, family, and friends, and she would be happier returning to her old way of life. She had a wonderful time with me, would always remember me, and wished me the best in life. It would have been a believable "kiss off," and I would have dropped the matter. Instead, she told a story that didn't make sense and then compounded it with lies. Her behavior simply generated my continuing pursuit of the truth.

I thought of the saying: Oh, what a tangled web we weave, when first we practice to deceive!

She acted like a criminal who wanted to be caught. The entire story she told me in November was a fabrication. She had been on the cruise ship. She had never been to France. She was not scheduled to go to Eastern Europe. The phone call was not from her tour-guide employer. The coup de grace was her telling me—with tears running down her face and dabbing at her eyes—that she loved me, would always love me, was still my wife, would always be my wife.

How was it that Rachel could be so mendacious toward me when I asked nothing from her but to share

INVESTIGATION OF RACHEL

my life with her and make her happy? I was willing to commit a sizeable part of my net worth to help her if she had cancer. What sort of human being was I dealing with who would lie to me under these circumstances without any apparent motive or personal gain? It was beyond my comprehension.

I thought I might be dealing with some form of mental illness, but I didn't know what. The closest diagnosis I could find in the DSM (the Diagnostic and Statistical Manual of Mental Disorders published by the American Psychiatric Association) was a Borderline Personality Disorder (BPD). This is described in greater detail later. I was not comfortable with this diagnosis. People with a BPD usually mellow out by their early forties and are generally very unstable. Rachel was over fifty and had maintained stability with me for over five months. In addition, prior to meeting me, she was gainfully employed by the Olympus Cruise Shipping Line for four to five months; they rehired her when she ended the relationship with me; she successfully worked for them another four or five months and was scheduled to work on their flagship for the winter. This didn't fit my picture of a BPD, but I couldn't find anything else to describe her personality.

Now, frankly, this development with Rachel had left me emotionally disturbed; I needed psychiatric help. My mind was caught in a reverberating circuit—oscillating between the two Rachel's I knew. I couldn't make a nexus out of it. I had never heard a story like it. My sense of betrayal and confusion was profound. My anger toward Rachel was without boundary.

RETURN TO FLORIDA, DECEMBER 1992

I left Boston in early December and drove to my condo in Florida.

I knew the Piraeus was due at Fort Lauderdale on December 20th. I decided to visit the ship on that date. It was possible that the Olympus was mistaken, perhaps Rachel was not on the ship. I wanted to give her the benefit of any doubt. I didn't want to jump to a conclusion without supportive evidence. Just in case, I had prepared a letter telling her that I knew of her ruse.

When the ship docked, I inquired of one of the staff who had disembarked if Rachel was on board. He indicated she was, and I gave him a letter to bring up to her. He later brought it down stating that Rachel had disembarked in Barcelona. I knew he was lying since he had earlier told me she was on board the ship.

I spoke to a social hostess who had come down to greet the disembarking passengers. She claimed she never heard of Rachel. Again, I knew she was lying—she said something about maybe she was in a different section or department on the ship. The average person is a poor liar.

INVESTIGATION OF RACHEL

I observed the original staff person I spoke with, the social hostess, the ship's port agent, and a member of the Port Authority all huddled together. It was obvious they were discussing me. In the meantime I asked a number of disembarking passengers whether they had seen Rachel that morning. They told me they had.

Finally, the man from the Port Authority approached me and asked me to leave. I don't know what Rachel told them about me, but it was obvious I was viewed as a nefarious character. I asked to see the ship's port agent to give him a letter. There was no objection to this. I walked over to the agent and asked him if he would deliver the letter to Rachel. He said he would and I left.

When I returned to my condo, I wrote a detailed description of my relationship with Rachel. I concluded that Rachel had a BPD. I made an appointment with a forensic clinical psychologist; and prior to the appointment, I asked her to read the story. I do not have a background in clinical psychology— my academic experience was in physiological and experimental psychology—and I have no clinical experience. I felt I needed the insight of a specialist.

The psychologist felt that the most prominent feature of Rachel's personality was that of a sociopath. There were some borderline features, but the sociopath was the main feature. The former name for sociopath was psychopath, and the current name is anti-social personality.

The psychologist went on to explain that the key to the diagnosis was Rachel's truthlessness without any motive. According to the psychologist, the salient feature of the sociopath in relationships was the con. The con itself was the "high" and any personal gain was secondary. That was why the sociopath's behavior was so confusing and why the sociopath is so successful in the con. People can often see through a con because they sense the other person is trying to gain something. With the sociopath there is no apparent gain. To receive pleasure out of inflicting pain on someone without a motive makes no sense to the average person. The victim of such a con is devastated. Their reality testing is questioned. They become very distrustful of other people. Depression is common. Suicidal feelings may develop. The victims feel violated at the deepest level.

I found the diagnosis of sociopath difficult to accept. First, generally men are sociopaths not women. Second, sociopaths do not return money and other items of value. Third, the area of love is generally profound, sacrosanct, and too complex for a woman to engage in a con. It is not that women walk on water in relationships with men, but to fake obsessional love without personal gain for five months would be considered most unusual.

I remained uncomfortable with the psychologist's diagnosis, so I made an appointment with two local

INVESTIGATION OF RACHEL

psychiatrists. Both took the position that they couldn't make a diagnosis without speaking with the patient. One of the psychiatrists stated that the behavior described could very well be a variant of normal behavior. He suggested I watch some of the "soaps" on TV. Rachel's behavior was not so unusual compared to the behavior of some of the women on TV soaps. The other psychiatrist thumbed through his copy of the DSM and thought that Rachel could be a sociopath, borderline, narcissistic, histrionic, manic depressive (bipolar), or dependent personality. Both psychiatrists seemed more concerned about their fee than helping me. I was unimpressed with the psychiatrists.

I returned to the psychologist and told her about my experience with the two psychiatrists. She said she wasn't surprised.

The psychologist and I discussed Rachel back and forth for about seven or eight sessions. She remained confident about her diagnosis. She explained to me that Rachel had sensed my vulnerability on board the ship. Sociopaths are like that. Their antennas pick up on another person's emotional pain. I was still mourning for my mother, and Rachel sensed I was needy and vulnerable. She carefully nurtured the relationship until she had her claws firmly into me. Only then did she drop me. The entire relationship was a con. Rachel got a "high" or thrill from the con. The psychologist admitted she never heard of a sociopath returning money. This was the one unusual feature of the story. According to the psychologist, I was not the first man Rachel did this to and wouldn't be the last.

I finally accepted her diagnosis. In so doing, I was plunged into a state of a deepening emotional turmoil. What sort of evil monster was Rachel? How could a human being do this to someone with a serious heart condition?

I related the following story to the psychologist. I said I felt like Rachel was a woman dressed in white —a Florence Nightingale figure—who found me in a depressed state and nursed me back to health. Once I was able to stand on my own two feet, she removed her outer garments and revealed a Nazi uniform. She then took a gun and pointed it at me. I cried out— why are you hurting me? She replied, I am not hurting you, but us. And then she shot me twice, turned around, and walked off leaving me for dead.

The psychologist's explanation was a double-edge sword for me. It gave me a diagnosis but left me in turmoil. I struggled reconciling the Rachel I traveled with and the sociopath diagnosis. I felt not merely betrayed but in disbelief that someone would engage in such a perfidious attempt to hurt someone who only wanted to make her happy. I felt more than anger; I felt maniacal rage! I described my rage in these terms: I imagined taking a sword and decapitating her, then cutting her arms and legs off, and finally chopping her torso in quarters. Even this frenzy would not placate me. I would then take her dismembered body and send individual parts to each of her sons and sister. This, of course, was a reverie only. In real life I am a non-violent person. Acts of violence, even gunfire, scare me.

The psychologist mentioned she knew of a male psychiatrist who was semi-retired. He had been her mentor when she was studying for her Ph.D. She had taken the liberty of discussing my case with him. He only took unusual cases. She asked me if I would be interested in meeting him on a social basis. I answered in the positive.

She arranged for me to meet him in her office one evening. She excused herself, and we were left alone. I thought this was strange: I was supposed to meet him socially. In any case we spoke. He indicated he had read my story, concurred with the sociopath diagnosis, and found my case interesting and a challenge. He asserted I took a passive posture, spoke of being vulnerable, depicted myself as a victim controlled by others, when in fact the opposite was true. My passivity and vulnerability was a ploy; with my intellect I controlled the next person. When I decided it was in my interest to assert myself, I did so. He sensed in my person a state of controlled rage.

I agreed to meet him again. The psychologist and I decided he should handle my case. After the second session he told me his fee was one hundred

RACHEL'S BURNING BUSH

dollars per session, and he accepted cash only—he didn't take insurance. His body signaled tension when he said this.

This bothered me. I sensed something was wrong. Something told me that he was not licensed and couldn't bill an insurance company directly. In addition the way I was manipulated from one therapist to the other unsettled me.

I went over to the psychologist's home and spoke with her. I asked her if he was licensed to practice in Florida. She said he wasn't. She was bothered by the fact that he tried to bill me directly. She stated it wasn't right for me to have to pay him when my insurance paid her. He should bill under her name. She would have to speak with him. She feigned anger. (I thought to myself she was being untruthful—he was seeing other patients in her office, she knew what he was doing, and he knew the proper procedure.)

Then the plot became deeper. She then told me that they had been married once. He forced her into bankruptcy. She was practicing as a psychologist in Louisiana—the only state with a Napoleonic-legal-code system. He had made some real-estate investments, had a heart attack, and the investments went sour. Under the law in Louisiana, she was held responsible for his debts. She lost everything.

I canceled my next appointment with her ex-husband. The thing smelled in more ways than one.

INVESTIGATION OF RACHEL

I noted she was a chain smoker (she never smoked in the office) and heavy wine drinker.

The situation became even more macabre. I discovered, through my contacts in the area, that her ex-husband wasn't a psychiatrist at all. He was a psychologist, and he wasn't licensed to practice in Florida; nor was he a member of the American Psychological Association. I also discovered that she was not licensed to practice in Louisiana. She held a Georgia license. I thought to myself, just my luck, another Rachel.

Needless to say my experience with the shrinks in the State of Florida left much to be desired.

Now I was on my own. The experience with the psychologist didn't really bother me, but it certainly didn't help. In the course of my business career and personal life I have been lied to, deceived, and cheated —that is all part of living. Why should the mental-health field be any different? In addition, I do not view professionals—whether they be physicians, attorneys, psychologists, CPA's, clergymen, or engineers—as icons. If they make a mistake or exhibit aberrant behavior, I accept it as human. I only resent when they think they are something special and speak ex cathedra.

As I indicated I am not a physically violent type, but I am vindictive (sometimes viciously vindictive) when hurt. My modus operandi is to attack in a non violent way—generally using the legal system. In

RACHEL'S BURNING BUSH

Rachel's case this was not possible.

The first thing I did was write to the captain of the ship on which she was sailing. The communication with the captain was not meant to be vindictive. In the covering letter I explained I had a relationship with Rachel about a year ago which ended rather abruptly. I had consulted a psychologist who had diagnosed Rachel as a psychopath who engaged in a cruel con with men. The psychologist had felt this was a pattern of behavior. I wasn't the first, and I wouldn't be the last. Rachel was probably using her position on the cruise ship as a front to seek out her next victim. I had suffered great pain from the relationship. I was writing him in the hope that he could prevent a recurrence of this activity. Attached to the covering letter was the story I had written and submitted to the psychologist. The story was written in clinical terms without affect. It was a factual report and stayed clear of personal or emotional attacks.

The second thing I did was write to Mark Jackson, president of the cruise line in Miami. The letter was similar to the letter sent to the captain. I stated that Rachel was probably using her position on the Piraeus as a cover to dupe other United States passengers. I felt the Olympus had a responsibility to its passengers to prevent a recurrence of such activity. Attached to the letter was the same account I had sent to the captain.

INVESTIGATION OF RACHEL

I anticipated a response from Mr. Jackson. What I expected to receive was a public relations letter thanking me for bringing the matter to his attention, assuring me such activity was inconsistent with the philosophy of the Olympus, and asserting the well being of the passengers was of utmost concern to him.

When I heard nothing, I phoned Mr. Jackson. He knew who I was and had read my report. He was taciturn and guarded on the phone. He told me the reason he hadn't responded to my letter was that I hadn't asked for an acknowledgement. He said it was none of my business what the Olympus intended to do about my letter. It was a corporate matter. His tone was acrimonious and defiant. It didn't make any sense. Why was he acting this way? What was he covering up? I said to him it sounded as if he didn't care at all about the passengers. He responded with some disingenuous remark about how the Olympus appreciated my business.

I found the conversation unsettling. I wrote him a second letter, a copy of which follows. I never received a reply.

RACHEL'S BURNING BUSH

LETTER TO OLYMPUS CRUISE LINE

February 23, 1993
Mark Jackson
President, Olympus Cruise Line, Inc.
Miami, FL 33105

Dear Mr. Jackson:

    I found your phone response regarding my letter concerning Rachel enigmatic and part of the mystery surrounding this affair.

    I wrote you for one purpose only: viz., to make sure that another American passenger was not duped by Rachel and as a consequence suffer financial loss and psychological pain.

    There was no animus in my letter toward Rachel or your company.

    The specifics of what you do and how you handle this are indeed your business. But where is your PR sense? Don't you care at all about past, present, or future passengers?

    For your information the letter I wrote you is being expanded into a non-fiction book as well as being adapted into a screen play. Since the Olympus Cruise ships will be an integral part of the story, you might want to reconsider your stonewall response. If you desire to expand your phone statement, please do so in writing by April 1, 1993.

Sincerely,

INVESTIGATION OF RACHEL

LETTER TO RACHEL AND HER FAMILY

The third thing I did was vindictive. It was aimed at hurting and embarrassing Rachel. It also had as a purpose correcting any misinformation in my story and hoping to elicit Rachel's side of the story. I wrote to Rachel, her sister Leah, her son Jacob in Syria, her sons Isaac and Abraham in Spain. There was a short cover letter and the same account I had sent to the Olympus. The only response to my letter was from Leah who wrote to my brother Esteban in Boston asking him to make me stop communicating with Rachel. Esteban just threw the letter away and did not mention it to me. A copy of my letter follows.

To: Leah, VA.
Isaac and Abraham, Spain
Jacob, Syria
Rachel, Piraeus

We have a saying in los Estados Unidos: You reap what you sow (Galatians 6:7).

The enclosed story represents an in-depth outline of a non-fiction book which is being adapted into a screen play.

If you desire to rebut any of the facts or conclusions, please do so in writing by April 1, 1993. Sincerely,

RACHEL'S BURNING BUSH

TRIP TO GALVESTON

The fourth thing I did was also vindictive. It was also aimed at hurting and embarrassing Rachel. But at the same time it had another purpose—additional information gathering. I didn't understand how a person could continue to function as a social hostess and at the same time have such serious psychiatric problems.

I had, even before meeting Rachel, planned an automobile trip through the deep South including the Panhandle of Northern Florida, Alabama, Mississippi, Louisiana, Arkansas, Tennessee, and Texas. The Piraeus was due in Galveston, Texas on March 17th. I planned a trip so that I would be in Houston on March 16th. Galveston is fifty miles from Houston.

My plan was to speak with some passengers who were embarking on a trip on the Piraeus, tell them about the psychologist's diagnosis of psychopath, and elicit their observations about Rachel's behavior on the ship. The account that I had written for the psychologist would be given to the passengers. I was interested in any additional information they could supply me. I also envisioned the possibility of this causing discomfort to Rachel.

But an unexpected thing happened.

INVESTIGATION OF RACHEL

GALVESTON, TEXAS MARCH 1993

When I arrived in Galveston, I parked my car in a lot across the street from the Steamship Company. I took an elevator to the second floor of the Steamship Building. As I was walking over the crosswalk to the area where the passengers gathered to board the ship, I met Rachel and a female friend walking in the opposite direction. Rachel was as much surprised to see me as I was to see her. I hadn't considered the possibility that she would leave the ship and spend time in Galveston. In any case Rachel spoke in Spanish to her friend, and her friend left. She invited me back to the passengers' lounge to talk. Before sitting down with me, she first went up to a member of the ship's staff and spoke with him.

My impression of Rachel was that she didn't even look like the woman I knew. She had not cut her hair in over a year. She had lost about twenty-five percent of her body weight and didn't look well at all. She always wore eye make-up—the only make-up she ever wore. Now she wasn't even using eye make-up. She was physically unattractive and dressed in nondescript clothing. She did not look happy or content. Although she had been cruising for four months, she did not have a tan. She looked tired.

I thought to myself that Rachel looked like the victim here. She certainly didn't look like a woman in love—in the back of my mind I had always considered the possibility of another man in the picture. This thought was reinforced by her telephone call from a man at 7:30 A.M. in November when I was visiting her.

In contrast I was dressed in a white, tennis-type outfit, had a good tan, and had put on a few pounds. I looked to be in robust health, felt at ease and spoke calmly. I certainly didn't look like or act like a victim.

For the first time since I knew her, I spoke with her from the vantage point of knowing I was interacting with a mentally-ill person. Instead of accepting what she said as valid, I filtered whatever she said as coming from a pathological liar.

Rachel had received my report about the psychologist's diagnosis. She was aware that I knew of her ruse. She knew I had communicated with the Olympus and with her family.

I shall try to describe the highlights of our conversation. During my discussion with Rachel, I acted as a clinician/detective rather than a duped lover. I was fishing for information, emotional responses, and inconsistencies.

She again repeated she still loved me, would always love me, and was still my wife. This was said without emotion and sounded disingenuous.

I moved slightly closer to her on the sofa. She responded by moving away from me.

I asked her why, if she still loved me and was still my wife, she wasn't with me. She replied, she

INVESTIGATION OF RACHEL

couldn't live with me. I was mentally ill. She realized now that I never loved her. What I really wanted was a translator and someone to take care of me. When I had no more need for her, I sent her home. I abandoned her when she was sick. I was a bad man.

I reminded her of my offer to take care of her financial expenses if she had cancer. She responded that the offer was not sincere. I wouldn't pay for her cholesterol treatment and refused to pay five thousand dollars for her health insurance. I did not argue with her.

Rachel stated that I had hurt her terribly. She had given everything she had to me. (At least during the time we were together, I would agree with this last statement.) She was afraid of me; I was a dangerous man.

And suddenly out of the blue she asked, "Would you take me back?" I blinked, thrown momentarily off guard. The thought crossed my mind: "Are you crazy?" Before the words came out of my mouth, I stopped—realizing how ridiculous such a question was. Instead I asked her if she would like to come back. She didn't reply initially. I repeated the question. She answered that she considered coming back when I visited her in Spain. I answered her original question by saying we would have to talk about it.

We engaged in small talk. Throughout our conversation it was clear that she was continuing to lie to me or to contradict past statements. Her lies were of no importance. She denied ever saying her husband had discovered latent homosexual feelings. She denied saying her mother had ever beaten her. She maintained she had never been a tour guide but went directly to the cruise ship. When I asked her about her letter postmarked from Seville, Spain, which was nowhere near where the ship cruised, she had no answer.

I asked her why she had lied about being a tour guide, when in fact she was a social hostess on board the Iliad. She replied, she didn't want me to know where she was.

At some point in the conversation, I asked her if she remembered the game we used to play. I reminded her I would point to a chair or some other elevated object; she would stand up on the chair; I would then give her a great big hug; and she would smile and laugh with glee. Upon being reminded of this, Rachel stood up, clapped her hands to her ears, and cried out I was tormenting her.

She was either unraveling before my eyes or a great histrionic actress putting me on.

We left the passenger lounge, walked back across the crosswalk, and entered an elevator. As I pressed the button for the ground floor, she jumped out in an agitated state. Fear, very close to terror, registered on her face. She was afraid of being in the elevator with me. She told me she would meet me downstairs.

INVESTIGATION OF RACHEL

We spoke awhile in the parking lot. She grew increasingly angry and uncomfortable. I tried to calm her but was unsuccessful. I bent down, put my hands on her shoulders, and attempted to give her a friendly goodbye kiss on her cheek. She pulled back in real anger and snarled not to touch her. Her enmity was intense.

Finally I said to her: "Rachel, you do not look well. You look physically ill. Do you have cancer?" She did not reply.

She is five feet two inches. She weighed about one hundred forty-five pounds when we traveled together. She appeared to now weigh around one hundred ten pounds. Her face was very thin. Her belly flat. Her skin color was poor. Her eyes were listless.

I told her that if she were ill and needed help, I would do what I could for her. Shortly thereafter she just turned away without a word and walked off.

I went back upstairs to the passengers' lounge, but I had no stomach for speaking with the passengers about Rachel. I had my closure. I really did not know what was wrong with Rachel, but that wasn't germane to me anymore. Clearly she was not happy. She was a jumble of conflicting emotions. She was in misery and in tumult.

It was out of this misery that she caused me so much misery (misery likes company). I had seen myself as the victim—and of course I was—but the real

RACHEL'S BURNING BUSH

victim was Rachel. She was her own worst enemy.

It is a trite but true statement that when someone causes another person misery for no reason, it is a reflection of the person's own internal misery; and conversely, when someone feels good, the person brings sunshine into the lives of others.

As I reflected on the labile emotions demonstrated by Rachel and what could be considered borderline psychotic behavior, I wondered if this had been a charade and a clever hoax. How was it possible for someone to be an effective social hostess and be so mixed up? Someone so disturbed would certainly act out on board the ship. How could she sustain normal behavior for four months on board the ship and act so non compos mentis with me? How could someone change emotional states so abruptly? How could someone change from obsessional love to complete avoidance so suddenly? How could someone change from a social hostess, to a psychotic and back to a social hostess in such a short period of time? How could someone so unstable be so well liked by so many people? Where was the missing piece? What had I overlooked? What false assumptions had I made?

As I stood up to leave, still absorbed in my thoughts, a gentleman approached me and addressed me by name. He looked to me to be an official from the ship. He identified himself as Captain Washington. I thought perhaps he wanted to discuss Rachel with me. He appeared friendly, and we chatted as I walked toward the passenger exit. As we approached a side door in the passenger lounge, he politely asked me if I would step inside to discuss a matter with him. I thought this was a strange request, but I went inside.

When we both had seated ourselves, he took out a badge and told me a complaint of harassment had been made against me; unless I left immediately, he would arrest me. I was stunned and confused. I began to speak, and mentioned I was leaving when he interdicted me. He interrupted me and told me not to talk, or he would arrest me on the spot. He went on to say that under Texas law harassment was punishable by incarceration.

I was not only scared and intimidated but actually in fear of my life. He was a big man, appeared unstable and spoke to me in a menacing manner. The image flashed through my mind of police arresting men on some of the TV shows. They handled people roughly. I was concerned that, with my heart condition, rough treatment could result in my death.

I sat silently afraid to speak, leave, or make any move which would cause him to lose control and go over the brink. He acted like a ticking time bomb about to explode. He spoke with me for probably no more than ten minutes, stating he would let me go this time because I was from out of state; but if he ever found me here again, I would be arrested for harassment, no questions asked.

I accompanied him downstairs. In the parking lot I was stopped by a Galveston police officer who alleged that I had grabbed Rachel. This was becoming serious! I had no idea what was going on. I asked him from whom he had heard that information. He told me the parking-lot attendant told him. I went over to the parking-lot attendant and asked him if he told the police officer I grabbed Rachel. He said, "No." He had told the officer I put my hands on her shoulders (which I did). The police officer came over. I told him the attendant mentioned nothing about grabbing Rachel. He responded in anger by threatening to arrest me if I did not leave the parking lot immediately.

I saw no point in escalating this any further. If this had been my home state, I would have gone over to the police station and filed a complaint. I was on a pleasure trip and decided the only sensible thing to do under the circumstance was to leave without further incident. Arguing with street police is a no-win situation.

Before leaving Texas I researched the law on harassment. In Texas, harassment is defined and covered by the state's penal code 42-07. It is very specific. It has to do with letter writing and phone calls. There is nothing that I did in Galveston which could have been interpreted as harassment as defined by Texas law. Texas at that time did not have an anti-

INVESTIGATION OF RACHEL

stalking law; although even if it did, I can't imagine that such a law would apply to my activity.

LETTER TO CAPTAIN WASHINGTON

I wrote to Captain Washington for an explanation of his behavior. A copy of the letter follows.

May 19, 1993
Captain Washington
Galveston, Tx 77553

Dear Captain Washington:

On March 17, 1993 you advised me that a complaint of harassment had been made against me and you enjoined me to leave the area.
You made it clear that you didn't want to discuss the matter. Since I was from out of state (Florida), I was easily intimidated and feared incarceration if I challenged you.
I request detailed information on the complaint made against me. I assume it was either Rachel and/or personnel on the Piraeus. Who made the complaint? What specifically was alleged? What Texas penal code was alleged to have been violated?
I look forward to your reply. This matter makes no sense to me. I would like to understand, from the

RACHEL'S BURNING BUSH

point of view of the person who made the complaint, what specifically I was alleged to have done which you felt constituted harassment.
Sincerely,

Captain Washington never replied.

LETTER TO RICHARD WARD

I then wrote to Richard Ward, Captain Washington's superior. A copy of my letter and his reply follows.

May 25, 1993
Richard Ward
Galveston, Tx 77550

Dear Mr. Ward:

Reference the enclosed letter to Captain Washington which has not been answered. I wish to know who made the complaint of harassment against me? What specifically was alleged? What penal code was alleged to have been violated? What specific part of the penal code was alleged to have been violated?

Captain Washington took me into a closed room, showed strong animus toward me, would not let me speak or tell him my side of the story, and advised me if I ever came to the area again he would arrest me

INVESTIGATION OF RACHEL

for harassment. It was very clear to me that he felt I was guilty of harassment.

I am first of all interested if the complaint came from the cruise ship or Rachel?

If there is a report on this matter, I would like to receive a copy.

If you cooperate with me and provide me with the information I request, no harm will come to Captain Washington or your company. If you do not cooperate with me, I will engage an attorney, bring legal action against your company, and using the discovery process force you to answer my questions. This may then escalate to civil and criminal charges against the officer and the company. At this moment in time that is not my intent.

I am telling you the truth. I did not engage in any act of harassment or anything that remotely suggested harassment. I had not come to visit Rachel. I was as surprised to see her as she was to see me. She invited me back to the passenger lounge to talk and at no time mentioned anything about my bothering her.

What Captain Washington was not aware of was that he was set up. He, as well as your company, are bit players in a complex international matter. Answer my questions and remove yourself from this matter before it engulfs you. The plot is much thicker than you have any idea.

Sincerely,

Mr. Ward wrote back indicating that his company was not involved in any dispute I had with anyone. I was present on company property without effective consent. I stated my desire to leave. I was escorted from the premises and departed. He regarded the incident as closed.

It is clear that Captain Washington stonewalled me, and Richard Ward lied to me. They were both protecting themselves from possible civil suit. Both the Galveston police officer and Captain Washington were not following proper police procedure. The police officer had no authority to order me off a private parking lot at which I had paid to park. Captain Washington did not know the Texas law on harassment and was way out of line in his behavior toward me.

DISTRICT ATTORNEY OF GALVESTON

Since I received no satisfaction from writing to Captain Washington and Richard Ward, I wrote to the District Attorney in Galveston and asked him to investigate the matter.

The District Attorney wrote me that when Rachel returned to the parking lot, she complained to two local Galveston police officers. A police officer from the company was also present. Rachel alleged that I had harassed her and had a history of following her from port to port and harassing her. The company police officer communicated, by radio, the nature of

INVESTIGATION OF RACHEL

the complaint (no formal complaint was made). Captain Washington, inside the corporate headquarters, heard the complaint on the radio and proceeded to stop me as I was leaving the building. (I was in the main waiting room of the building; there were no signs or guards indicating this was private property; the public came and left at will.)

The District Attorney answered another question. The Olympus was not involved in the complaint. Because of the stonewall response I had earlier received from the president of Olympus, I did not know if somehow the cruise line and Rachel were involved in some criminal activity. The District Attorney's response satisfied me that the matter involved Rachel alone.

BOSTON, SPRING 1993

When I returned home to the Boston area, I was still puzzled by the Rachel affair. There were too many inconsistencies. I remained puzzled by her weight loss. I consulted a number of psychiatrists and psychologists in the Boston area to gain some insight into Rachel's behavior. They all felt that she was not a psychopath. Most felt she had a borderline personality disorder. Some felt she had a narcissistic personality disorder. One psychologist felt I represented a "demon lover" to Rachel—that I had taken possession of her soul and she had to avoid me at all costs. Another felt the problem was a post-traumatic-stress disorder.

I consulted a specialist on Borderline Personalities. I asked him to read the same report I had prepared for the Florida psychologist. After reading the report he stated that Rachel probably was a woman with a BPD and in torment. She did indeed love me; but she had to avoid me, because I couldn't be trusted. I abandoned her when she was ill. If I could abandon her once, I could do it again. She couldn't trust me. The weight loss was associated with depression not organic illness.

I reacted with a sense of guilt.

There is a major difference between a psychopath and borderline diagnosis. The psychopath commits anti-social acts and is indifferent to the suffering he inflicts on others. His emotions are usually flat, although when it suits his purpose he can feign what he considers the appropriate emotion. While considered mentally ill, he is essentially an evil person. The borderline, on the other hand, is in torment and is emotionally labile. She is mentally ill, but she is viewed in more sympathetic terms.

I wouldn't do anything to hurt Rachel if she was in torment. In view of what I had just been told, I felt the letters I had written indicating she was a psychopath were obtuse.

Around this time I had an echocardiogram done by my cardiologist. He informed me that I might have a clot within my heart. He advised me to have an MRI done to verify this. The condition was treatable with blood thinners. Nevertheless, the idea of a clot within my heart frightened me. If it broke loose, it might cause a stroke or a fatal heart attack.

In response to what the psychiatrist had told me, I called Rachel and apologized to her for stating she was a psychopath. I informed her about my cardiac problem. She said she was sorry to hear that, but her affect was flat. I told her she could call me in a few days if she was interested. She stated she would not call me. If I wanted to call her with the results, I could. I was left with the impression not of love, but rather of total indifference—she couldn't care one way or the other. I didn't matter to her at all. When I went back to the specialist on borderlines and told him what had happened, he said that she probably wasn't a borderline. Unless she had found another lover, and there was no indication she had, her behavior upon learning about my heart problem did not sound like a borderline to him.

There was one bit of information that remained unanswered: the weight loss. Was this due to depression or was it organic in nature? I had wanted to visit the Holocaust museum in Washington, D. C. Rachel's sister, Leah, lived only twenty-five minutes away in Virginia. I decided to kill two birds with one stone.

In early June 1993 I visited the museum in the

RACHEL'S BURNING BUSH

morning and then drove to Leah's house in the afternoon. As I pulled up to the house, Leah was returning from work. She pulled into the driveway. As she walked to her house, I exited from my car and walked toward her. I asked her if she knew who I was. She responded by calling me by my first name. We spoke briefly in a friendly manner. I asked her if I could speak with her for a few minutes. I anticipated speaking with her outside the house. Instead, she invited me into her house to speak. As we proceeded to the front steps of her house, her teen-age daughter arrived from work, and the three of us went into the house and sat in the living room.

I told Leah I had unexpectedly met Rachel in Galveston, Texas. Rachel appeared to have lost thirty to forty pounds and looked to be in ill heath. I told her such a weight loss was generally associated with either depression or a major medical problem. I asked Leah if Rachel was medically ill. She said she wasn't. I asked if Rachel had experienced any psychiatric problems in her youth. Again a negative answer.

I then told her about my Galveston experience with Rachel. As I told the story, Leah's face changed. Initially her face had been neutral and passive, but slowly a Dorian Gray metamorphosis took place, her lips tightened and twisted, her eyes registered hostile emotion, and her body registered discomfort. The story disturbed her. I had the sensation of déjà vu. This was just what happened with Rachel in Texas: I

INVESTIGATION OF RACHEL

was politely invited to sit down and talk; the initial talk was pleasant; and then slowly, anger surfaced and mushroomed.

Leah mentioned she did not know much about her sister. They had lived apart during their adult years and communication was infrequent. The last time she heard from Rachel was a short note from Galveston. She didn't know Rachel was back in Spain.

Finally her suppressed affect surfaced. She claimed the purpose of the letter and story about Rachel that I had sent to her in January was to hurt her. The letter was even addressed to Mr. and Mrs. _____rather than to her. What did her husband have to do with this. Instead of writing her a thank you letter for the hospitality she had extended to me by allowing me to stay at her house, I wrote a letter whose only purpose was to hurt her. But she got back at me, she exclaimed. She wrote a letter to my brother Esteban, including a copy of my letter and story, to show him the type of man I was. She asked Esteban to have me stop bothering Rachel. My brother discarded the letter and never brought it up until I asked him about it.

Why she wrote to Esteban was unclear. Esteban said he received a short note only; no story was attached. Why didn't she write directly to me? In my letter to her I stated that if she disagreed with anything I had written, she should write to me.

Leah ended the conversation by saying that she

hoped I made a million dollars on the book—that the only purpose I had in writing the book was to make money. I told her I was not in need of money and was not writing the book for that reason. I was not writing the book to hurt Rachel or her family. I certainly had no intention of hurting her (Leah).

I apologized to Leah for any pain that the write up caused. I told her it was not my intention to harm her.

As I left her home, I felt uneasy. It was like re-experiencing with Leah what I had experienced with Rachel. I could understand if she were suspicious of me; I could understand if she were hostile to me for writing a pejorative characterization of Rachel; but it seemed to me to be narcissistic, egocentric, and paranoid to think that I wrote the report to hurt her. Why would I want to harm her? What importance was she to me? It was Rachel that had hurt me, not Leah. The report was about Rachel, not Leah. Leah's name was not even mentioned—other than stating Rachel had a sister in Virginia.

I remembered I used to call Rachel the president of the Avilda Meshuggener Society. I concluded the sisters were both members of the same society. There were a number of parallels in the behavior of Rachel and Leah. Both communicated with my brother Esteban rather than me. Both invited me to sit down and talk and then turned on me. Both exhibited friendly to neutral behavior initially which changed to hostility and anger without apparent reason. Both felt I was a bad man. Both exhibited psychopathology. Siblings frequently display similar psychiatric behavior. My meeting with Leah appeared to support the diagnosis of psychiatric rather than organic reasons for Rachel's behavior.

Another thought crossed my mind. Perhaps this wasn't narcissistic/paranoid behavior. Perhaps in reading my report, hidden suppressed memories were brought back. Perhaps some traumatic event, which both sisters witnessed or experienced, was behind this. Leah, in reading my report on Rachel, recognized what was happening within Rachel. It brought back memories of that trauma. In sending Leah the report, I brought the trauma back to her conscious memory and caused her much pain. Leah recognized that somehow I was the agent that triggered this repressed memory in Rachel. That is why she told me to stay away.

PSYCHOTHERAPY

I decided to seek some psychotherapy to help me resolve my fixation on Rachel. During the summer of 1993 and early fall, I saw a psychologist twice weekly. I did a lot of reading on personality disorders, the psychology of women, and self-esteem. I also consulted with other psychologists and psychiatrists. I was slowly working my way through my fixation on

RACHEL'S BURNING BUSH

Rachel. One day I had an epiphany.

I had renewed a past relationship with a female friend. I noticed that she would be sweet and pleasant ninety percent of the time; but ten percent of the time, she would get cantankerous without any reason; or if there was a reason, her affect was disproportional to the stimulus. One day I called her up at her office during her lunch hour, and she was cold and hostile to me. This was more than just having a bad day at the office. When I hung up the phone, I realized that it was possible for normal functioning people to have two opposite personalities. Someone or something can trigger the second personality. I had been struggling with trying to establish a connection between the Rachel I traveled with, the Rachel who worked on board the ship as a social hostess, the Rachel who lied to me in Spain, and the Rachel who exhibited such jumbled emotions in Texas. The epiphany I experienced was the realization that within some normal functioning individuals two opposite personalities can exist. One doesn't have to be psychotic or have multiple or split personalities to have this dichotomy.

While it seems so simple and obvious, this perception allowed me to significantly reduce my fixation on Rachel. I had been caught in a quagmire of my own false thinking: someone couldn't carry on normal social functioning, then exhibit borderline-psychotic behavior, and then return to normal

INVESTIGATION OF RACHEL

functioning. I had assumed more integration in an individual's personality. I had assumed that there would have been a spill over from the psychotic behavior during the time the individual was behaving normally. I had assumed that during normal periods the individual would exhibit from time to time behavioral problems. While I was aware of the concept of splitting (which I will explain later), I thought it applied to psychopathological states not between normal and psychopathological states. The splitting of the self (which will also be explained later) occurs at two levels in some people: (1) during the aberrant behavior, and (2) between the aberrant and normal periods.

One of the consulting psychologists suggested I put a notice in the paper to see if other men might have experienced a similar ending in a relationship.

SUDDEN ENDINGS - OTHER MEN

I put an ad in the Boston paper: "Males wanted who have experienced a sudden ending in a stable relationship with a female. Author, writing a book on subject, would like to hear from you. Call _____."

I received over fifty calls. The calls were helpful to me in understanding that I was not alone, and my reaction was not unusual. What I found unusual was the depth and duration of pain experienced by the men. A number of men cried and became so choked up they couldn't talk. One man stated that his breakup occurred ten years ago, and he was still in pain. A number of men mentioned being in pain over five years. One man, a clinical psychologist, said he had a sudden ending of a relationship almost at the altar. Ironically the woman who left him was herself a psychologist. It had happened six-months ago, and he still was in terrible pain. For the first month he was unable to function, he was deeply depressed, and experienced suicidal thoughts. None of his friends were helpful. People told him to "get on with your life and find another woman."

Again and again I heard the same stories. The men withdrew from social contact, became distrustful of others, and couldn't bring themselves to date again. If they did date, there was a barrier between them and the woman they dated. The emotional pain they experienced was worse than a death, because this pain lingered for years. Thoughts of the woman were omnipresent. Most of the men had eventually gone into therapy to deal with the lingering pain. Many of them felt disappointment in therapy. Everywhere they turned, they heard the same tune: what is wrong with you; why are you letting this woman control your life; pick yourself up, act like a man, find yourself another woman, and stop feeling sorry for yourself. The relationship is over with. Stop thinking about the woman; she doesn't want you, accept that.

The problem that these men had—and that I

had—was that few people had ever experienced a sudden ending in a relationship involving a soul mate. The men had felt that they were going to spend the rest of their lives with this other person. They had no inkling of any problem. There had been no deterioration in the relationship, no major fights, no signals. Just bang! It's over with. Most people have had endings in relationships. Most relationships, however, go through a series of stages where there are fights, disagreements, communication problems and misunderstandings. By the time the relationship ends, enmity exists on both sides. The average person, in listening to the tale of sudden endings, interprets the ending based on personal experience. They cannot understand why the person is in so much pain.

I have come to learn there are three types of sudden endings. In so called normal people, there is almost always someone else in the wings. People do not normally end a relationship, unless they have someone else. Another type of sudden ending involves current abuse—short term or long term, betrayal of trust, a con where someone is duped out of money, or a major trauma or set back. The third type of sudden ending involves a person with a major psychiatric problem. This person may end the relationship suddenly without someone else in the wings, without current abuse, betrayal of trust, profit, motive, major trauma or set back. The individual's behavior is often associated with, or traceable to, major childhood

RACHEL'S BURNING BUSH

trauma or abuse.

Almost all the calls I received from men involved a sudden ending in a long-term relationship and another man in the wings. There were signals, but men appear to be more trusting than women. If a woman stays out late, the man accepts her story. If the reverse were true, the average woman would be suspicious.

One of the men I spoke with claimed to have known women like Rachel. In fact he claimed his cousin was just like Rachel. He said such women are usually middle aged. They can be found around piano bars or as social hostesses on cruise ships. They go where they can meet lonely, middle-aged men. They are attracted to two types of men. One is a man of high integrity who will treat them well and buy them things; the other is a man who just uses them for his sexual pleasure. They are totally uninhibited sexually and will satisfy any man's fantasy. When they become involved in a meaningful relationship with a man, they are a man's dream. They are wonderful cooks, maintain the house in spotless condition, and treat the man as the most important person in the world. They sense what the man wants, what is important to the man, and satisfy his every wish. They can tolerate about five or six months of this. During this time the man, without being asked, gives the woman money, and buys her clothes and jewelry. He might even set her up in business (and ultimately loses his entire

INVESTIGATION OF RACHEL

investment). The man can't believe how lucky he is. He has found a soul mate. And then the woman leaves suddenly and disappears. She may lay low for a while, visit one of the men with whom she has had a short relationship (she has a stable of men she visits for a short period of time), or she may go back to looking for another man at either the piano bar or on the ship as a social hostess. She doesn't need to work since men give her money and take care of her. The men who become involved in a five-to-six-month relationship with such a woman are psychologically destroyed by these women. If the man asks for his money or jewelry back, the woman returns it. When the woman is in these longer-term relationships, she really experiences love; but then she tires of the relationship and moves on. Because she is not acting but really experiences love, the men are totally convinced of her sincerity. When she leaves, the men are left not knowing what hit them. Their sense of reality is shaken. These women appear and act entirely normal. They rarely go to a psychiatrist or psychologist, because they don't see that there is anything wrong with them. For the most part the mental-health field has no direct knowledge of these women. Frequently, these women begin to act this way after a traumatic ending in a marriage. Generally they are between the ages of forty and fifty-five.

Some of the men I talked to had considerable insight into their pain and its enduring quality. When someone whom you love dies, there is a grieving process; but your love and memory of such a person does not die. You visit the grave if you wish; you talk about the departed with family; you think of them on special days—birthdays, anniversaries, date of their death, special holidays. When there is a divorce, it is frequently preceded by a stormy period of fights, which serve to break the bond of love. By the time the divorce comes, most couples are bitter toward one another. The period of soul-mate feeling has long past for both. One remembers the person not in love but with enmity. The pain one feels is associated with negative feelings toward the other person. When there is a sudden ending in a relationship, one of the parties is caught in a state of love and must grieve for that person and forget about them. Such a loss therefore is much more difficult than the loss from death; because with a sudden ending, you are required to forget about the person.

PSYCHOLOGISTS AND PSYCHIATRISTS

In order for me to help myself with closure, I felt the need to understand who Rachel was. I didn't know which way to grieve. Had I been the victim of a con? If so, anger was the appropriate response. Was Rachel in turmoil and deeply mentally ill? If so, compassion might be the appropriate response. The picture was very confusing. There seemed to be two

INVESTIGATION OF RACHEL

Rachel's in operation. One was a kind, loving, caring happy woman with whom I traveled; the other was a manipulative, mendacious, ruthless woman who could invite me to sit down, tell me she loved me, and then after we parted complain to the police that I was harassing her. How was it possible for someone to either be so wicked or so mentally ill and still be able to function as a social hostess? How does someone go from a state of love and wanting to go everywhere with her lover, to a state of total indifference toward her lover, within a matter of two weeks of returning to Spain?

I had begun my investigation by seeking insight from psychologists and psychiatrists in the Boston area. Many of them were of no help at all. They had never heard a story like this. A few seemed to think Rachel had a borderline personality disorder, but there were parts to the story that didn't fit the picture. They felt the story in Texas represented splitting—which is a defense mechanism associated with borderlines. Splitting refers to seeing someone as good one moment and bad the next. The professionals were of the opinion that she really did love me, but at the same time she felt that I was a dangerous man who could harm her. On the other hand her total indifference to the possible clot in my heart was indicative of a lack of love. The following is a list of the various explanations I received from mental-health professionals with whom I consulted.

RACHEL'S BURNING BUSH

1. An unknown factor. Something may have happened when Rachel returned to Spain which may have directly impacted on her subsequent behavior to me. I found no evidence to support this position.
2. She felt inadequate and uncomfortable in her role as my wife. Her problem with English, my life style, my friends, my interests, my high expectations of her as my wife—created tensions within her and feelings of being unworthy. She ended the relationship to regain her self respect. While I do not discount this as a factor, there is too much chaos and mendacity to support this simplistic explanation.
3. She used me! She saw me as a rich American who could provide her with an easy life. After a time, she realized the effort she had to make was not worth the price she had to pay. She tired of me. She dropped me ruthlessly and returned the money, jewelry, and clothes to sever all ties with me. She set her sights on bigger fish. The business about loving me was an act. I discount this theory as well. There is too much chaos and tumult in her behavior, and too much fluctuation in her weight, to be consistent with a cold, calculating woman, someone putting on an

INVESTIGATION OF RACHEL

act, or an adventuress.

4. She is a psychopath (antisocial personality). The con was the high. Lying is a prominent feature of the psychopath. I reject this theory on a number of grounds: psychopaths do not return money and their behavior generally is more controlled and less jumbled than that demonstrated by Rachel.

5. I am her demon lover. This was suggested by a Jungian therapist. Rachel was obsessionally in love with me. She merged with me and lost her identity. She felt totally under my control. I was like an addiction. Once she returned to Spain and was free of me, she sought to distance herself and regain her identity. It was a matter of survival for her. She couldn't resist me. While this is a very interesting theory and offers an explanation of Rachel's behavior, it doesn't answer the question of why she fell obsessionally in love with me. Nevertheless it is a novel theory.

6. Rachel has a borderline personality disorder. The splitting in Rachel's attitude toward me is suggestive of this diagnosis as well as the abandonment issue. The origin of this disorder is

thought to be fear of abandonment by the maternal figure or parental abuse. The borderline patient suffers from low self-esteem and generally chooses a lover who is strong and powerful, merges with that individual, and uses her lover's strength to fill the emptiness and worthlessness she feels about herself. When her lover disappoints her, she feels abandoned and rejects her lover. This is the diagnosis favored by the majority of professionals who have read the story. I discuss this disorder in greater detail later.

7. Rachel's behavior is suggestive of a variant of a complex post-traumatic-stress disorder. This theory focuses on the etiology of the behavior. According to this theory, Rachel's behavior is based on severe abuse or trauma in childhood. The likelihood of sexual molestation should be considered. The trauma impels people like Rachel to seek out close relationships and then to withdraw from them. The terror of the trauma intensifies the need for protective attachments, but closeness reminds the person of the trauma. The traumatized individual alternates between isolation on one hand and clinging to others on the other hand. The dialectic of

the trauma results in the formation of intense, unstable relationships that fluctuate between extremes. The victim seeks powerful authority figures who will take care of her. She idealizes the person. She is haunted by the fear of abandonment or exploitation. Inevitably, the chosen person fails to live up to her expectations, and she then denigrates the same person she recently adored. Defense mechanisms commonly break down in the third or fourth decade of life, often associated with a life trauma such as a death or divorce. Only then does the underlying fragmentation become manifest. This theory is the newest theory to explain the type of behavior exhibited by Rachel. According to this theory childhood abuse, parental alcoholism or mental illness, divorce, death, or abandonment can also produce a "push-pull" behavior in relationships. The person desperately seeks love and companionship, and then feels engulfed and retreats fearful of being hurt again. The person in effect is recapitulating the original problem.

RACHEL'S BURNING BUSH

PRIVATE DETECTIVES

It was now August 1993. I was unable to obtain closure from my discussions with professionals in the mental-health field. It was clear to me this was a dead end. The lingering pain was becoming a nuisance. I needed to take a different course. The thought crossed my mind that perhaps this wasn't a psychiatric problem at all. Perhaps Rachel was involved in some international matter involving money laundering, drugs, or information gathering. In any case I decided I needed more information. I decided to take more direct action.

In order to fill in some of the missing pieces of this story, I engaged a private detective in Greece to contact the Olympus Cruise Company and provide me with an employment background on Rachel. I actually had to engage two different agencies because the information Olympus provided was inaccurate. In fact both agencies obtained inaccurate employment information. Sifting through both reports, however, I came up with the following information.

Rachel was a hard-working social hostess and interacted well with passengers. She was not involved romantically at any time with either a member of the staff or any passenger. She was not a drug user. She did not have any major medical or psychiatric problem. She was honest and did not engage in criminal activity.

She was, however, considered moody and had

INVESTIGATION OF RACHEL

outbursts of anger and arguments with the staff.

After leaving me and returning to Spain in April 1992, she probably did take a job as a tour guide. This was a point of confusion on my part. Rachel originally told me she was a tour guide and never went back to work for the Olympus. In Texas she claimed she never was a tour guide but went back to work directly for Olympus. The private detective was able to ascertain she went back to work for the Olympus on July 10, 1992. The letter she sent me in June 1992 was from Seville, Spain. (The Olympus Cruises do not go near Seville.) It is therefore safe to conclude that she took a job as a tour guide after leaving me in April 1992 but before rejoining the Olympus in Greece in July.

On March 25, 1993 (I saw her on March 17th), she left the Piraeus in Texas or the Caribbean and flew to Greece to join the Omega owned by the Olympus. She stayed until the end of May 1993 when she was asked to share a cabin as the ship was full. She created a fuss and refused to share a cabin. She then moved her suitcase and belongings to the deck and said, "Either I get a cabin by myself or I leave now!" Since this was not possible, she quit and flew back to Spain—leaving the ship without an assistant social hostess.

The report(s) answered or confirmed the following: (1) There was no other man involved. (2) The date she returned to work at the Olympus after leaving me. (3) In superficial relationships with passengers she was outstanding, but with close, long-term relationships with the staff she exhibited anger and was moody. (4) The exact nature of why she left the Olympus. The reason given is vintage Rachel. If she does not like something, she abruptly changes her behavior, disassociates herself from the offending person or situation, and will not listen to reason.

The private investigator in Spain was asked to do a background check on Rachel. This was a much more complete investigation than the employment check done by the Greek detectives. The following facts were obtained: Rachel and her family left Chile in 1975 and went to Germany. Rachel left Germany in 1979 and went to Spain. Her husband worked for a pharmaceutical company from February 1981 until the time of his suicide in January 1987. Her neighbors and friends spoke very well of Rachel and her family. There was no evidence of any major psychiatric or medical problem or criminal activity on the part of Rachel. There was no evidence of promiscuous activity or drugs. She lives a quiet life.

Her work history in Spain was irregular, working a few months, then being unemployed for many months. This may be consistent with the life of a tour guide or it may reflect a behavior pattern involving a lack of commitment over a sustained period of time. It may also reflect difficulty in finding employment in Spain or being privately employed.

One piece of information surprised me.

INVESTIGATION OF RACHEL

Following her husband's death, Rachel purchased her condo with insurance money she received. After buying the condo from the developer, she contacted an engineer who told her there might be something wrong with the heating system. She spoke with the developer about the problem; but instead of asking him to correct the problem, she demanded thirty thousand dollars to keep quiet and not tell anyone. This overt blackmail attempt was a side of Rachel that I had never observed. In fairness to Rachel, this is one man's word. I do not know if it is true.

The first private investigator I hired was not fully successful in his surveillance of Rachel. He noted she did not work. She spent time around the condo or shopping. She had regained her lost weight. She lived alone with her son. She noticed she was being watched and angrily reported the detective to the police forcing the investigator to discontinue his surveillance.

I hired a second private investigator to complete the surveillance. The second private investigator was also noticed by Rachel and reported to the police. He found this to be very unusual, noting that people are not normally on the alert unless there is a reason.

A third private detective was hired in the summer of 1993 to finish the investigation. He determined that around January of 1994 Rachel took a private position as a companion to an elderly woman at a salary of around $1,000.00 a month. Her widow's pension was around $1,000.00 a month. Her mortgage payments were around $500.00 a month. By being careful with her money she could make ends meet.

By October 1993 the pain from the sudden ending with Rachel had lessened considerably. When I had returned to Florida in November, I had settled on the theory that childhood sexual trauma was the underlying cause of Rachel's behavior. I didn't know whether it was incest or rape.

HYPNOTHERAPIST

The local Sunday paper carried a story about a hypnotist who was involved in therapy with incest survivors. I consulted this woman, read her my story, and asked what she thought. She felt Rachel was a victim of childhood sexual molestation of some form. She sent my story to an associate who also agreed with that position.

The hypnotist asked me if I would like to act as a consulting psychologist for her group. I explained I did not have a Ph.D. and was not a licensed psychologist. She thought, however, my background in psychology plus my caring nature would be helpful to the women in her group.

As I listened to the horrible stories of sexual and physical abuse these women told, I found the insight that had escaped me. One of the women stated she still loved her father. "A father is someone special,"

INVESTIGATION OF RACHEL

she explained. But she was also very angry at him and hated him for what he had done to her. She wanted nothing to do with him and couldn't care if he lived or died. I had always heard that love and hate could coexist, but I had never heard that love and total indifference could coexist. This is what this woman was voicing. It was what Rachel was saying to me and which made no sense to me. I now understood. Rachel was recapitulating in disguised form a childhood trauma. It involved love, fear, anger, hate, banishment, and punishment of the perpetrator. I was the substitute for the perpetrator. She was reenacting in disguised form an unresolved conflict from her childhood. I had been a bit player in her life story.

I had made the mistake of assuming Rachel was reacting to me. <u>By substituting the perpetrator for me, Rachel's behavior makes perfect sense.</u>

The stories the women told involved intergenerational abuse. One woman told of her grandmother being a prostitute in South America. Another woman told of her grandfather being an abusive alcoholic and wife beater. The cycle is clear. Perpetrators are themselves victims who in turn victimize their families. Perhaps this was what was also meant by the biblical admonition that the sins of the fathers will be visited upon the children to the third and fourth generation (Exodus 20, Fifth Commandment).

Prior to hypnosis these women related feeling a

jumble of emotions unconnected to anything. They had a lot of anger which they took out on family members. They knew something was wrong; they were in emotional turmoil inside; but they did not associate it with sexual trauma. The linkage between the trauma and the intense floating emotions had been repressed. Hypnosis had enabled them to bring to consciousness the repressed trauma. (The women in the group read my story about Rachel. They identified with parts of the story and felt that she was a victim of childhood sexual abuse.)

CHILDREN OF HOLOCAUST SURVIVORS

One lingering question remained unanswered. Rachel was the daughter of Holocaust survivors. Was there any connection between her behavior and the fact that her parents survived the Holocaust? There is a whole field of literature on this subject. I sent my story to a psychologist who specialized in treating children of such survivors and asked him for his opinion. He indicated that he had never head a story like the one I presented and saw no tie in with the Holocaust.

CHAPTER 6: CONCLUSION

After considering the limited facts at my disposal, I concluded that Rachel was a deeply wounded woman whose behavior was probably caused by some trauma in childhood. I do not know what that trauma was. I suspect it was sexual in nature and involved sexual molestation. Beyond that I do not wish to speculate.

I could be wrong of course. The conclusion could represent self-deception, an attempt to mask rejection and save face. But I am inclined to think otherwise.

Rachel was over fifty years old and yet her emotions were childlike. This is what people found so endearing about her. I misjudged her personality. I thought her behavior reflected a cultural difference: women from South America are apt to be subservient. In retrospect I think Rachel's behavior reflected an arrested emotional development. She was still operating emotionally from the period of the childhood trauma.

I believe Rachel did love me and was happy when we were together. Pictures taken during our travel consistently showed her with an ear-to-ear smile. Some of the pictures, taken by others, showed her looking up at me with adulation. I do not believe this was a con.

The hallmark of trauma in a non-psychotic individual is the holding of two contradictory beliefs or emotions. Love and hate are not contradictory

RACHEL'S BURNING BUSH

emotions; they are the flip side of the same emotion. But to say you love someone and at the same time not care if that person lives or dies—that is a contradictory statement. They are mutually exclusive. And that is what Rachel was saying to me.

People who are traumatized in childhood have a compelling need to find a strong, benevolent spouse whom they can trust and who will take care of them. There is nothing unusual in that emotion. But the traumatized individual is afraid of intimacy. She both yearns for it and is terrified of it. In her mind it is linked with the original trauma: trust and a violation of that trust. People like Rachel are caught in a dialectic—a struggle between opposite forces.

Rachel's life was marked by major disappointments. When she met me, she desperately wanted this relationship to work out. She made extraordinary efforts to realize her goal. During the course of our travels, I disappointed her—especially with my frustrations. When I sent her home for medical tests, she felt abandoned. This was enough for her to end the relationship.

The ending of the relationship really caused her great pain. Her weight loss was probably associated with depression. Part of her continued to love me. But I had become a demon lover who had to be avoided.

The incident in Texas appears to me to be a disguised form of a re-enactment of the original

CONCLUSION

trauma: Affirmation of love, terror at being closed in an elevator, screaming not to touch her in the parking lot, and finally going to the police to keep me away from her.

In simple terms, this story is a tragedy. Two people who loved one another deeply, who caused one another great pain and misery, and finally separated. I do believe that Rachel suffered as much as I did.

While I doubt I will ever forget this relationship, there is a happy ending to this story. During the summer of 1994, I met a woman from Ecuador on board a cruise ship to Alaska. We were married on February 18, 1995. While my new wife's personality is similar to that of Rachels—happy, nurturing, caring, loving—there are important differences. My wife is a deeply religious woman; she has very close family ties; she is well-educated (a social worker with two master's degrees); she holds a supervisory position and earns a high salary; and she/we are able to discuss our feelings/differences, validate and understand one another, and reach compromises when necessary which are in our mutual best interest. We both feel we have found soul mates and have made a commitment for life. We are both very happy.

There is light at the end of a tunnel!

APPENDIX

RACHEL'S BURNING BUSH

THE AUTHOR'S NAME

Lucho	The Author's first name is actually Louis. In Spanish the name Louis is changed to Luis. In Chile the nickname for Luis is Lucho. When I traveled in Chile, I was called Lucho.
ben	In Hebrew this means son of. A variant of this is Bar Rab or Bar Reb, both of which mean son of the scholar. (Bar means son; Rab or Reb means scholar.) Scholarship is highly prized in the Jewish religion, and one honors one's father by referring to him as a scholar.
Alexander	Is my father's first name.

Because of the personal nature of this book, I chose a pseudonym. In the Jewish religion it is the practice to name a person in Hebrew by using the Hebrew first name, followed by the expression "son of," and ending with the Hebrew first name of the father. My Hebrew name is actually Eliezer ben Yitzhak or Eliezer bar rab Yitzhak. A female would use bas or bat instead of ben. Bas or bat means daughter of.

APPENDIX

TITLE

The title "Rachel's Burning Bush" was chosen for a number of reasons.

As explained in the beginning of the book, Rachel called me her "Burning Bush." In effect saying I was her God.

But, it is unclear from the title who is the subject of this book. Is it about Rachel or is it about me. This ambiguity was done on purpose.

Also, embedded in the title is an elusive dialectic. Rachel's original perpetrator was probably a familial male. He was her original "Burning Bush." A man whom she loved, but who violated her. She was tormented by the opposing emotions she felt toward her violator.

Later in life, she sought out men of authority who would protect her and in whom she could trust. As she merged with these men, the feelings from the original dialectic surfaced, and she was forced to separate herself from these men. Her life is a re-enactment of the original trauma.

Ironically, she imprinted on me her experience. I was caught in a dialectic. I was tormented by trying to make a nexus out of the good Rachel I knew and with whom I traveled, and the other Rachel who surfaced in Spain and in Galveston. Part of my brain was fixated on the Rachel I experienced, and part of my brain was able to understand the dynamics of

RACHEL'S BURNING BUSH

Rachel's experience. They represented mutually exclusive pictures. This was the basis of my torment.

Rachel's original perpetrator, although I never met him, traumatized me.

As you can see, the title of the book has a talmudic dimension to it. Who was Rachel's Burning Bush? What was meant by the expression Rachel's Burning Bush?

ANALYSIS

ANALYSIS

Most people are aware of the phenomena of middle-aged men leaving their wives for younger women. Sometimes this occurs suddenly in an apparently happy marriage. In such a case the behavior of the husband is frequently incomprehensible: up until the moment of leaving, the man is a loving, caring husband who just days before might have made an unusual gesture of love and affection toward his wife. On closer analysis of these cases, the man has often experienced a recent major set back in his career or some other major loss. The man's identity is tied into the loss or set back. His self-esteem system rests on external accomplishments. He abandons his wife and attempts to start life anew with a younger woman. The diagnosis of such men is often Narcissistic Personality Disorder.

When I interviewed men who had experienced sudden endings, a number of characteristics about the women emerged. They generally came from dysfunctional families with a high incidence of alcoholism. In almost all cases the women left to go with another man. In many cases these second relationships did not last long.

Another common unstable relationship is found in people in their early twenties to thirties. It is marked by falling madly in love very quickly, elevating the lover to the status of deity without fault, and then after a few months or perhaps a year devaluing the person suddenly and ending the relationship. Another lover is frequently in the wings. Such people are frequently diagnosed as having a Borderline Personality Disorder.

The story about Rachel does not fit any of the above profiles. Something else was at work here. I believe it is found within the female experience. It is necessary to begin with what it means to be an infant and child.

An infant sees itself as the center of the universe and strives for power to satisfy its needs. This egocentricity and power assertion reaches its zenith around the age of two when the child is most outrageous and demanding. Somewhere between two and three the child begins to identify as a male or female.

If the child is a female, she begins a life long process of identification and attachment to her mother. She learns what it is to be female from her mother. She learns that females are nurturers and caregivers and must suppress their own needs for the good of the family. Mothers take care of children and their husbands. Daughters are expected to help their mothers and suppress their own needs to satisfy their mothers. They learn they exist in relationship to other people. The egocentricity which was part of their earlier life gives way to a sense of self which is based on relations with others. The female child learns a sense of dependency on others.

If the child is a male, he begins a process of separating from his mother. In the process of learning to become a male, he learns to devalue that which is associated with being female. He searches for his father to learn how to be a male. In most cases in our culture the father is relatively unavailable. He is out working or absent. Without a father to identify with, the son learns to be autonomous. Feelings are suppressed. To be a male means to be independent of others and leads to isolation. He learns to compete with other males, rather than share intimacy as females do with other females.

The sex hormones begin to increase in puberty and reach their apex in adolescence. Estrogen in the female and testosterone in the male not only are responsible for the secondary physical sex differences but also serve to heighten the psychological differences between the sexes. In oriental philosophy this is expressed in yin-yang theory. The yin is female and seen as passive, negative, dependent, obedient; the yang is male and seen as active, positive, independent, creative.

Cultural expectations further divide the sexes. Emphasis is placed on the female's beauty and body proportions. Her sense of self and identity comes not from achievement, but from her ability to compete with other females for a male's attention. Males, on the other hand, gain a sense of self and identity through power, money, and achievement. Those that succeed are able to attract women of beauty.

The male and female enter the adult world with a different sense of self. The female is incomplete without others; the male is autonomous and sees others as an appendage of himself or to gratify his needs.

When the male and female marry, she seeks someone of power to make her complete, someone to merge with, and someone to take care of her; he seeks someone of beauty to feed his ego, someone to protect and dominate, and someone to take care of him.

Later, around the time of the male and female menopause (age fifty), estrogen levels fall off in females and testosterone levels decrease in males. The psychological differences begin to become less pronounced. Females become more independent and aggressive; males often mellow and experience soft and tender emotions.

Often around this time, males and females experience an existential crisis. The female's beauty has begun to fade, her children are grown, and her identity and purpose in life are subject to soul searching. The male, likewise, questions the futility of his striving for power, money, and achievement. They have not brought him happiness. He, like the female, has bought into a false system. He has worked so hard for his family that his family hardly knows him. His wife is going out to work, or has been out working,

ANALYSIS

and doesn't need him anymore.

The self continues to grow throughout life. As children we are still dependent on our parents and are still egocentric. In a healthy environment the parent nurtures the child's sense of self, encourages the child, and makes the child feel loved. The child's sense of self grows. The child learns a sense of interdependence with others.

In an abusive family environment something very different happens. In severe abuse, where a threat of life is involved and a state of helplessness exists (incest, severe beatings), the child commonly dissociates during the period of abuse and the mind splits off from the body enabling the victim to endure the pain. If the child is a male, he frequently remembers only the event and not the emotions associated with the event; if the child is a female, she is apt to repress the memory of the event and be left with the emotions associated with the event. In both cases the abusive parent becomes the center of the child's universe. The true self fails to develop. Instead, a false self develops to meet the challenge of the abusing parent. Frequently the child attempts to become "extra good" or does everything right in hopes of curbing the parental abuse. This is one side of the false self. The other side of the false self is the internalizing of the abuse and developing a feeling of being bad or inadequate: the child thinks if he/she is abused, he/she must have caused the abuse. The child concludes he/she is bad. The self therefore instead of growing, arrests and splits into a good and bad false self. Sometimes the good self is presented to the world (this is shown frequently in superficial relationships), and sometimes the bad self is presented to the world (often surfaces in family settings).

A similar process may occur in childhood rape: dissociation, false self, and repression of memory of the event.

Abuse can take many forms. It can be verbal or physical abuse or abandonment. The result is generally low self-esteem which is really at the core of the false self.

In severe abuse the person develops defense mechanisms to deal with the tension brought about by being an imposter (false self). The specific defense mechanisms include projection, projective identification, primitive idealization, splitting, denial, distortion, and acting out.

Projection means attributing ones feelings and wishes to another individual.

Projective identification involves depositing unwanted aspects of the self into another person and manipulating the other person to experience feelings similar to one's own.

Primitive idealization is a mechanism by which objects are viewed as all good, omnipotent or ideal, while the object's badness is greatly exaggerated.

Splitting divides objects into all good or all bad

ANALYSIS

and features shifting from one extreme to the other. Sudden and complete reversal of feelings about a person may occur and may involve repetitive oscillations.

Denial is as the name implies: denial of the event.

Distortion involves reshaping reality to satisfy inner needs.

Acting out is a defense mechanism in which the individual expresses unconscious wishes through action. It also involves blaming others for one's behavior.

There were two other parts of Rachel's personality which appeared pathological: anger disproportional to the stimulus and mendacity.

Some of the reasons for anger include: (1) protection of self, others, group, institution or property, (2) personal or group gain, (3) helplessness, rejection, powerlessness, inability to change the other person to your position, (4) betrayal, (5) feeling threatened—physically or psychologically, (6) physical or psychological pain, (7) violation of expectations, (8) violation of beliefs and values, (9) feelings of being used, cheated, or taken advantage of, (10) displacement—anger really meant to be directed at someone else, (11) psychopathic or unknown reason, (12) organic: tumor or hormonal, and (13) defense mechanism germinating from false self.

Some of the reasons for lying include: (1) self deception, (2) self protection, (3) protection of others,

(4) personal or group gain, (5) fear or anxiety, (6) control and power, (7) manipulation, (8) pathological or unknown, and (9) defense mechanism germinating from false self.

One of the most confusing parts of my investigation had to do with the area of nosology or the classification of mental illnesses. The bible in the industry is the DSM or Diagnostic and Statistical Manual of the American Psychiatric Association. Unfortunately, mental illness is not easily categorized. The DSM leaves much to be desired, and there is much disagreement within the professions of psychiatry and psychology on the understanding and classification of mental illnesses. This is especially true in the evolving area of personality disorders. The DSM presents specific diagnostic criteria for each type of personality disorder it recognizes. The three personality disorders that might apply to Rachel include narcissistic, borderline, and antisocial personality. For each disorder there is a list of behavior patterns that fit that diagnosis. There is another school of thought on personality disorders that views these three personality disorders as defects of the self. Originally proposed by Kohut and further developed by "self" psychologists, this classification views these three personality disorders as narcissistic: with the narcissistic personality disorder the least narcissistic and the antisocial the most. (It includes the paranoid as even more narcissistic than the

ANALYSIS

antisocial.)

If asked to make a diagnosis of Rachel based on the information I had supplied, there seemed to be a feeling among the professionals with whom I consulted that the Borderline Personality Disorder (BPD) would be the closest fit.

The term Borderline Personality came into usage in psychiatry and psychology in the 1970's. It first appeared as a diagnosis in the DSM in 1980. The term borderline was coined to describe an individual who appeared normal, but would exhibit from time to time psychotic-type behavior, and then return to normal functioning. The person was neither neurotic nor psychotic but borderline psychotic. Some of these patients behaved normally for many months while others were unstable most of the time. Most of the patients were female. Therapists who treated them found them to be highly manipulative, and these patients developed a reputation as being difficult to treat and emotionally trying. Many therapists try to avoid treating such patients or limiting their practice to one or two such patients at any given time.

This is what the DSM lists as criteria for BPD:
(1) A pattern of unstable and intense interpersonal relationships characterized by alternating between extremes of over idealization and devaluation *
(2) Impulsiveness in areas such as spending, sex, substance abuse, shoplifting

RACHEL'S BURNING BUSH

(3) Affective instability *
(4) Inappropriate intense anger *
(5) Recurrent suicidal threats or self mutilation
(6) Identity disturbances *
(7) Chronic feelings of emptiness or boredom
(8) Frantic efforts to avoid real or imagined abandonment
(9) Transient, stress-related paranoid ideation or severe dissociative symptoms

The DSM requires at least five of the criteria be met. Those with * appear to apply to Rachel, but they number only four. Possibly the criteria of abandonment would apply to Rachel.

The "self" psychologists would probably view Rachel as a narcissistic-borderline personality. They would view Rachel as functioning adequately for long periods of time, acting out in a borderline psychotic manner for a short period of time, and then returning to adequate functioning.

Some of the psychiatric literature traces the origin of the Borderline Personality to fear of abandonment by the maternal figure. If the child is good and does what the mother says, then the child is rewarded. If the child disobeys the mother, then the child is threatened with abandonment. Rachel spoke of defying her mother and being beaten. The literature speaks of abandonment depression as central to the borderline's behavior. The self is poorly

ANALYSIS

integrated and there is a split and struggle between the good and bad self. The good Rachel is really too good. She is sweet, benevolent, servile, and unsophisticated. She is easy to like since she goes out of her way to please people. She functions well in superficial relationships. The bad Rachel is manipulative, cold, assertive, demanding, and difficult to deal with. She is defiant, angry, focused only on herself. The second Rachel manifests itself in areas of intimacy—personal and social.

According to this theory when Rachel returned to Spain alone, she saw this as abandonment and experienced abandonment depression. Rachel did appear to be depressed during the first week in April 1992 when she returned to Spain alone. To overcome the depression, she left home and took a job where she would be dealing with a lot of people. For people like Rachel there is security in groups.

One of the classic books on antisocial personalities is "The Mask of Sanity" by Hervey Cleckley. Earlier names for antisocial personality include sociopath and psychopath. Cleckley preferred using the term psychopath in his book and presented the following clinical profile of such people:

    (1) Superficial charm and good intelligence: The psychopath reflects robust mental health; he is free of neurosis or minor social or emotional impediments found even among the successful.

RACHEL'S BURNING BUSH

(2) Absence of delusions and other signs of irrational thinking.

(3) Absence of nervousness or psychoneurotic manifestations: cool under stress.

(4) Unreliable: Appears reliable in the short term, but in the long run he has no sense of responsibility, loyalty, or commitment.

(5) Untruthfulness and insincerity: Candor and trustworthiness seem implicit in the psychopath at all times. During the most solemn perjuries, the psychopath has no difficulty in looking someone tranquilly in the eyes. He is a pathological liar.

(6) Lack of remorse or shame: denies all responsibility.

(7) Commits antisocial acts in the absence of any apparent goal.

(8) Incapacity for love: The psychopath is very skillful at pretending love but is indifferent to the hardships he brings upon those for whom he professes love.

(9) Poverty in affect: The psychopath can become excited, enraged, weep, laugh, seem happy. These are expressions rather than feelings. They are artifacts—not real emotions.

(10) No insight: He blames his troubles on others. He is an individual who appears to have a sound mind but is more

ANALYSIS

incomprehensible than a psychotic patient. His is a true mask of sanity.

(11) Unresponsiveness in interpersonal relations: does not respond to kindness or trust.
(12) Fantastic and uninvited behavior with or without alcohol.
(13) Suicide rarely carried out
(14) Sex life impersonal: Sexual promiscuity is not uncommon.
(15) Failure to follow any life plan: The psychopath's sanity is in name only. By performance his conduct is that of the irrational behavior of the psychotic.

The DSM offers a different profile of antisocial personality than that described by Cleckley. There are many attributes associated with the DSM's description of Borderline Personality Disorder and Cleckley's description of Antisocial Personality Disorder that would apply to Rachel. The clinician could easily fall back on the diagnosis of Mixed Personality Disorder Not Otherwise Specified. I think there is a better diagnosis.

I made a fundamental error: I focused on the diagnosis of Rachel rather than understanding the underlying etiology. The DSM tends to do the same thing. It suggests diagnosis based on symptoms. In many cases that is appropriate. In some cases, however, the presenting symptoms mask the underlying etiology. It is the cause which should be the basis of the diagnosis. In the field of medicine sometimes physicians must use an empiric method of treating disease. This means treating the symptoms such as fever of unknown origin. Most physicians however would prefer to identify the cause of the fever and treat accordingly. The analogy applies to mental disorders as well. Unfortunately, the plethora of diverse symptoms that some mental disorders present makes diagnosis difficult.

The diagnosis I would apply to Rachel is the following: Delayed-Post-Traumatic-Stress Disorder of Unknown Etiology, most likely caused by repressed memory of childhood or adolescent sexual molestation, incest, or rape.

Some of the presenting symptoms for making such a diagnosis include the following:
- 45 years old or older
- Intense anger and rage that sometimes burst out unexpectedly
- Supersensitive to anger or perceived criticism by others
- Sudden reversals in emotional state without logic
- Mood swings, ranging from deep depression to overactive manic state
- Appears to be governed by emotions rather than reason
- Holding of two contradictory beliefs

ANALYSIS

simultaneously and accepting both of them
- Hyper-vigilance
- Non psychotic
- Gets along well in superficial relationships but has problems in familial relationships and long-term work relationships
- In intimate relationships with members of the opposite sex, she seeks powerful, benevolent authority figures who will take care of her. When the person chosen fails to live up to her expectations, she furiously denigrates the same person whom she recently adored.
- Pathological lying
- Tendency to be evasive and withhold information
- Recent life trauma such as death or divorce
- Highly manipulative of others

The hallmark of repressed trauma in a non-psychotic individual is the simultaneous holding and accepting of two contradictory beliefs which to the average person would make no sense. (I love you, but I don't care if you live or die.) Psychological trauma is an experience outside the average person's frame of reference. The seemingly contradictory beliefs held by the traumatized person do make sense if viewed from the trauma experience. Rachel's comments on one hand about loving me, always loving me, and on the other hand about never wanting to see or hear from me again or caring if I live or die seems to the average person to be nonsense. But her statements make sense if she is referring to someone whom she loved and who brutalized her. This phenomena of holding contradictory beliefs is similar to the defense mechanism of splitting and may be viewed as a variant of splitting.

    I reached the conclusion that the trauma was sexual because her problem areas are with men. She claimed her first husband, a Rabbi, had beaten her, locked her in her room and suffered from priapism (a very unlikely event since priapism requires medical intervention); she claimed her second husband, a physician, was unfaithful, committed suicide because he had discovered latent homosexual tendencies; I was a bad man, a dangerous man, a mentally-ill man who treated her poorly and abusively; and finally her attempt at blackmailing the man who sold her the condo.

    Trauma is usually reenacted or recapitulated in disguised form in intimate relationships. What happened in Galveston, Texas was, in my opinion, such a reenactment. "I love you. I am still your wife. You are a bad man. You are mentally ill. Will you take me back?" Jumping off the elevator in fear and terror of being shut in with me without a means of escape. Pulling back in anger when I bent down to give her a

ANALYSIS

goodbye kiss on her cheek. Finally having me punished by going to the police and telling them I was harassing her. In my opinion this represents in disguise form a recapitulation of some early sexual trauma.

Her indifference when I told her that I had a possible clot in my heart suggests familial sexual trauma: in effect saying to me that she loved me but couldn't care if I lived or died. This is the emotion that a victim has toward her familial sexual perpetrator.

I do not know what form this sexual trauma took. The story suggests a familial trauma such as incest or rape by a close family friend. It is possible that it might involve some other sexual trauma or even a non-sexual trauma such as severe physical beatings.

I know of only one anecdotal case similar to Rachel's story. The woman was gang raped in early adolescence. The trauma was blocked from her memory. She chose men of high positions in society, ruined them by leaking damaging evidence to their enemies, and then left them. She subsequently went into psychotherapy and eventually the source of her behavior was identified.

It is my belief that Rachel was hurt by this relationship with me. Because of sexual trauma being part of her history, I think she was easily seduced by me. The seduction process was within her, I made no attempt to seduce her. She found irresistible my gentlemanly qualities, my integrity, my intelligence, my soft, gentle caring nature, my ability to know and care what she was thinking and feeling, my quality of listening, validating, and giving positive feedback, and my financial ability to provide for her. Given this scenario, it is easy to understand how she fell madly in love with me before she really knew me. She was looking for a Prince Charming whom she could trust and who would take care of her. She was willing to do anything for that man.

As the relationship developed and the normal stresses of traveling were experienced, my complete personality showed itself. I wasn't the benevolent father figure that she found on the ship, but rather a man who reacted with anger and rage under certain circumstances, a man who liked to tease, a man with a history of past girl friends, a man who could send her home when she was ill. Because of her past background, she concluded I had misrepresented myself. I was a bad man; a dangerous man. I was like the man who was so kind and loving to her and then took advantage of her and deflowered or violated her. She had to avoid me at all costs.

Rachel's "Burning Bush" proved to be a false God. When a God is found to have feet of clay, he is banished or destroyed.

I do know that Rachel's perception of me and behavior toward me had very little to do objectively with me. I am neither an icon nor a devil. I was the

ANALYSIS

trigger from something in her past. I certainly never abused her psychologically or physically—that was in her mind. She gained my trust by demonstrating unconditional love and satisfying my needs. I tried to respond in like kind to her.

I loved her fully, tried to make her happy, and would have done anything for her. She was not my femme fatale; I could have parted company with her on an amiable basis and gone on with my life. I was not obsessionally in love with her. It was a comfortable, secure type of love. I loved her for her personal not her physical qualities or accomplishments. My obsession developed later as I tried to make sense out of this bizarre relationship.

While time tends to heal wounds, the memory of this traumatic relationship will not be forgotten.

It is my hope that (1) perhaps some woman reading this book might recognize some of her own symptoms and seek help, (2) some men who have lived through a similar experience will be able to understand what has happened and more readily go on with their lives, and (3) mental-health professionals when confronted with these bizarre stories will be able to understand, validate and assist their patients.

Women like Rachel are in emotional turmoil and pain. Anyone who gets too close to such a person can also suffer emotional pain—and that includes husband or lover or therapist.

Most therapists view people like Rachel as being

highly manipulative and very difficult to treat. People like Rachel have endured a psychotic-type experience. They appear normal, but their appearance is deceiving. They are from a different world with a different set of experiences. They can be helped by recognizing this difference and communicating and interacting with them accordingly.

BIBLIOGRAPHY

Bass, Ellen and Davis, Laura. *The Courage to Heal.* Harper. 1988.
Bennett, Madeline. *Sudden Endings.* Windsor. 1991.
Cleckley, Hervey M. *The Mask of Sanity.* Fifth Edition. Emily S. Cleckley. 1988.
Covey, Stephen R. *The 7 Habits of Highly Effective People.* Simon and Schuster. 1989.
Engel, Beverly. *The Right to Innocence. Ivy.* 1990.
Gray, John. *Men Are From Mars, Women Are From Venus.* Harper. 1992
Gunderson, John. *Borderline Personality Disorders.* American Psychiatric Press. 1984.
Haule, John. *Pilgrimage of the Heart.* Shambhala. 1992.
Herman, Judith Lewis. *Father-Daughter Incest.* Harvard University Press. 1981.
Herman, Judith Lewis. *Trauma and Recovery.* Basic books. 1992.
Jordan, Judith; Kaplan, Georgio; Miller, Jean Baker; Stiver, Irene; Surrey, Janet. *Women's Growth in Connection.* Gilford Press. 1991.
Kaplan, Harold and Sadlock, Benjamin. *Comprehensive Textbook of Psychiatry.* Vol. 1. Pages 375-376. Williams & Wilkins. 1989.
Kernberg, Otto. *Borderline Conditions and Pathological Narcissism.* Jason Aronson. 1985.
Kohut, Heinz. *The Analysis of the Self.* International Universities Press. 1971.

Kreisman, Jerold and Straus, Hal. *I Hate You - Don't Leave Me. Understanding the Borderline Personality*. Avon. 1989.

Leonard, Linda Schrierse. *The Wounded Female*. Shambhala. 1982.

Leonard, Linda Schrierse. *On the Way to the Wedding*. Shambhala. 1987.

Lowen, Alexander. *Narcissism. Denial of the True Self*. Collier. 1985.

Masterson, James F. *The Narcissistic and Borderline Disorders*. Brunner/Mazel. 1981.

Masterson, James F. *The Real Self*. Brunner/Mazel. 1985.

Peck, M. Scott. *The Road Less Traveled*. Simon and Schuster. 1980.

Sanford, Linda Tschirhart and Donovan, Mary Ellen. *Women and Self Esteem*. Penguin. 1984.

Stone, Michael. *Essential Papers on Borderline disorders*. NYUPubl. 1986.

ABOUT THE AUTHOR

The author received an A.B. in psychology from Brown University. His thesis—on cortical brain damage in children—was published in the Journal of Consulting Psychology. He served as a psychologist in the U.S. Army for two years and then attended Wesleyan University where he received an M.A. in physiological psychology. Based on his research, he published a number of articles in professional journals of psychology on "prenatal stress."

An asthmatic reaction to rat dander forced a career change. For a few years he worked as a psychologist in the space program doing research for NASA on vestibular-ocular interactions in a weightless environment.

He subsequently went to business school at Columbia University and worked for a few years as an industrial spy. Most of his career was spent as the president of a high-tech electro-optics company.

He retired in 1986 and pursued an indolent life for a number of years. In 1992 he returned to his first love—psychology. This book, which explores the mystifying behavior behind a "borderline personality," is the culmination of an intensive investigation over a two year period.

The author winters on the West Coast of Florida and summers in a suburb of Boston.